Praise for *Ho...*

"This book is a must read, not just contractors, but for all small business owners, and anyone on the team who takes part in hiring. As the owner of a recruiting company who works exclusively with small businesses, I can say with experience that *How To Hire The Best* is chock full of valuable and spot on information, tips, guidance, wisdom, and strategies to help you build a team that will take your company to the next level and allow you to have a business that supports you and the lifestyle you desire. I have seen it time and again!"

Erin Longmoon
CEO of Zephyr Recruiting

———

"If you own and run a construction or remodeling business, this book will change your life. I have personally witnessed how Dr. Sabrina's hiring and employee development strategies have transformed her contracting and remodeling clients' businesses and eliminated their employee headaches, as she teaches them how to hire A-Players who will help them grow a profitable business that runs smoothly. I am so excited that she is sharing her secret sauce in this book which is chock full of proven strategies, so that even more contractors and remodelers can benefit from her expertise and wisdom."

Donna Leyens
President and Co-Founder
Pumpkin Plan Your Biz

———

"As a business owner, your people are the way your business executes EVERYTHING. Attracting and retaining the best and brightest is the perennial challenge of all entrepreneurs at scale. That process starts with recruiting, and Dr. Sabrina Starling has delivered an in depth guide that will help you build a great team, all while juggling the multiple demands on your time as a business owner. She covers the broad strategy, the why, all the way down to the daily tactics that will make a huge difference in your company. I can recommend without reservation *How to Hire the Best* as a must read for those looking to grow and scale their hiring practices."

Rhamy Alejeal
Author of *People Processes: How Your People Can Be Your Organization's Competitive Advantage*, a 2018 Amazon #1 Best Seller in Human Resources
CEO of Poplar Financial

———

"In *How to Hire the Best*, Dr. Sabrina does a great job in providing a framework and practical steps for building a team of 'A-players.' Her ideas and suggestions are timely for helping contractors find and retain great talent."

Vicki Suiter
President & CEO Suiter Business Builders
Author of *The Profit Bleed*

———

"Finding top talent is one of the most important roles for a leader. This book offers a simple process to ensure you do just that."

David Burkus
Author of *Under New Management* and *Friend of a Friend*

"When Dr. Sabrina Starling told me she was writing this book I was ecstatic! With hiring qualified talent such a critical issue for so many contractors these days, this is a timely subject and I love Dr. Sabrina's approach to hiring 'A-players.' If finding great employees is a concern for you, this book is a must read."

David Hawke
AffluentContractor.com

"*How to Hire the Best* is a game-changer. No more playing small because you can't find A-Players! Dr. Sabrina Starling demystifies the challenges so many of us experience as we struggle to build champion teams. Her real life experience, rolling up her sleeves and getting in the trenches with her clients to solve employee problems, comes through in every solution she delivers. This book is full of real world, practical solutions to your hiring challenges."

Jeff McManus
Creator of Landscape University at the Jeff McManus Leadership Academy

------

"The first edition of *How to Hire the Best* went straight to my list of top ten books that entrepreneurs need to read to help them thrive and prosper. Now, Dr. Sabrina has done it again, with a revised, updated and expanded version, just for contractors who have the greatest hiring challenges! Dr. Sabrina Starling has taken one of the most contentious aspects of running a small or medium-sized business — finding, hiring and retaining top talent — and delivered a REALLY USEFUL handbook with insights, tips, hacks and strategies, which turn conventional hiring practices on their head. She writes lucidly and is obviously deeply connected to the clientele for whom she has created this book. Her experience with and empathy for small and medium-sized business owners jumps out from every page.

She has written this book for contractors and indeed her insights are invaluable to them. However, the lessons and strategies she describes are applicable to ANY small or medium-sized enterprise, irrespective of industry.
This book is a must-read for entrepreneurs anywhere."

Sir Steven Wilkinson
Founder & Writer-in-Chief
Good & Prosper Ltd.

———

Mike,

Thank you for all
your support of
this effort!

Sabina

Mike!

Thank you so much for all your support &

His effort!

Sylvia

HOW TO HIRE THE BEST

The **Contractor's** Ultimate Guide
to Attracting **Top Performing Employees**

Dr. Sabrina Starling

This book is dedicated to my girls
who inspire me to bring my best every day.

Table of Contents

Chapter 3
Attracting *Your* Ideal Team Members

Chapter 4
Where to Find Your A-Players

Acknowledgments

Since the first edition of *How to Hire the Best* was published, many of you have shared your hiring successes and setbacks with me. Through your successes, challenges and setbacks, as well as my own, I've continued to hone and refine this method. I greatly appreciate those of you who are on this learning journey with me, particularly those of you sharing your experiences within the book. With the publication of this book, you the reader, are now walking alongside us. I welcome your feedback and experiences in applying the Hire the Best System™ so that we can all benefit as I continue to refine it.

Thank you, Nick Pavlidis, for your work in developing the current edition. Your insights and perspectives have been instrumental in bringing this edition to life.

I greatly appreciate those of you who read this book prior to publication and offered specific feedback to improve the content. Thank you, Anne Compton, Linda Stapf, Christeen Era, Peggy Tvardzik, Mary Pierce, Geoff Fairfield and Richard Krebs.

Our team at Tap the Potential live and breathe this work daily as we support our clients in applying this method. Thank you, Darren Hopman and Stacey Seguin for your support and dedication to our clients' success. Thank you, Dona Krebs, for helping to manage the details behind the scenes as Tap the Potential keeps growing. Thank you to our Book Launch Ambassadors who are instrumental in spreading the word about How to Hire the Best, as well as our marketing team: Rochelle Rizzi of Le Vrai Nord, Cara Parrish, and the team at Cara Parrish Marketing, and Amy Marie of Heart and Soul Biz Essentials.

I also want to thank my good friend, colleague, and accountability partner, Donna Leyens, for supporting me through the ups and downs each week, and always having a good idea, no matter what the circumstance.

Most importantly thank you Mom and Dad, for always supporting and encouraging me, and in recent years, helping behind the scenes when there are more balls to juggle than I have hands to catch.

Introduction

Dear fellow entrepreneur,

You work excessively long hours. You shoulder high levels of responsibility for your team members, their families, and your clients and customers. You have your own family obligations. You juggle complexity on a daily basis.

The constant pressure of being tied to your business takes a significant toll on your health and well-being. As a psychologist, this concerns me deeply. As a fellow entrepreneur, I have lived this struggle.

I recognize you are working this hard not because you want to, but because you feel you have to do so. Who else can you depend on?

At the crux of this problem lies the biggest challenge facing entrepreneurs: Where do we find great people?

In 2016, I published the first edition of *How To Hire the Best*. That book solves this challenge with a system for attracting a steady stream of A-Players eager to go to work for you when you are ready to hire them. (A-Players are highly motivated, resourceful problem solvers in your business).

At that time, most of my clients were small business owners in rural areas—where there are more antelope than people. As you might guess, it's extremely hard to find top-performing team members in a rural area. There just aren't that many people to go around. I like a good challenge!

These business owners are hardworking and dedicated to their businesses, families, and team members—whom many consider family. Time and again, my clients would tell me they work seventy, ninety, and sometimes even more hours per week. Their spouses are frustrated with them. Their kids miss them dearly, wondering why their mom or dad works so much.

Disillusioned with the idea that owning a small business could help them achieve financial and life freedom, they resign themselves to doing what they know how to do: work hard. Disillusionment is topped by disappointment in themselves. They let their frustration and disenchantment boil over.

They lose their tempers at work and at home. Perhaps they check out emotionally from their families due to the constant distractions of work.

They are well-respected leaders in their community. Yet, they struggle. Many confide in me they wished they could go back to a simpler time, before they had team members. Maybe you can relate.

I wanted to help our clients overcome the employee challenges consuming their lives. So, I set out on a mission to use my skills as a trained psychologist and business strategist to help them solve their #1 challenge . . . how to hire the best team members.

I gathered top entrepreneurial thought leaders. I hired business coaches and interviewed successful business owners. This was to identify best practices for hiring exceptional team members and growing a thriving, profitable business.

I was dismayed to discover a lack of books written to help small business owners solve this challenge. Not only was there a dearth of books about this topic, but top entrepreneurial thought leaders confided in me they didn't have solutions either. I was tempted to give up. I was buying into the belief that as small business owner, we can't compete with the big guys for top talent. Then one morning, I awoke with a powerful question running through my head: *"What if it's not true?"*

That one question put me on a quest. I would find small business owners with great team members and ask them how they came to have those team members working for them. Sounds simple enough, right? Yet, no one would talk to me! Time and again, business owners told me a variation of this: "Sabrina, I have no idea how I got that person to work here. It was luck. If you find solutions to hiring A-Players in small business, please come back and tell me. I just don't know . . ."

Fortunately, I'm pleasantly persistent, and I kept asking questions. Those questions and the answers small business owners shared with me revealed patterns that I turned into a system. It reliably attracts top-performing team members regardless of your location or industry.

What resulted was the first edition of this book, *How To Hire the Best: The Rural Business Owner's Ultimate Guide to Attracting Top Performing Employees.*

In that first edition, I introduced a simple, structured system for attracting the best team members. Many businesses lack this system, and it keeps the owner stuck in the business. I've been humbled by the impact that first edition has had on the business owners it reached. Surprisingly, book sales continue increasing as word spreads.

For example, Misha and Kate Dickey, owners of the Good People Kitchen, used the Hire the Best System™ to fill a position they had been trying to fill for years. Before implementing this system, they were struggling to find good team members. They'd gone through a lot of team members. The lack of applicants and quality of applicants frustrated them. Using my Hire the Best System™, in just ninety days, they had a good team in place with applications continuing to come in. They were able to expand hours of operation to accommodate customer requests, and monthly revenue almost doubled. Best of all, they feel comfortable being away from the business and leaving it in the hands of their A-Players.

Amanda Henry, owner of Rainmaker Marketing Solutions LLC and WYHomeSearch.com also used my Hire the Best System™ to quickly hire three sales team members for her growing business. She commented, "Hiring was so much easier this time around!"

Todd Bussey, in rural Georgia, used the Hire the Best System™. He hired a new designer for his floral business within a few weeks of his current designer giving notice. He had multiple qualified applicants from which to choose. Before his designer gave notice, Todd had been working toward his business running without his daily involvement so that he could take a 4 week vacation. Without the Hire the Best System™ in place, Todd would have been pulled back in and abandoned his efforts toward that vacation.

Before the first edition of *How To Hire the Best* was even published, I began getting calls from business owners throughout the country. "I'm in New Jersey. I own a construction company. I can't find good help. Can you help me?" "I'm in San Francisco. I know we're not rural . . . can you help me?" "I'm in Denver. I'm drowning in work and can't find afford what my competition is paying their employees. Can you help me?"

Almost overnight, our client base expanded beyond rural business owners. Every business owner I've worked with has had hiring challenges that cause stress and undermine profitability.

I also noticed one group of business owners reaching out to me more than others, and in more desperation than others. They are in the construction industry.

Your challenges are greater than many other industries. Yet, there is tremendous *opportunity* for you when you solve your hiring problems.

The construction industry lost an entire generation of workers during the housing crisis in the late 2000s. When the housing bubble burst, construction halted across the United States and beyond. Many workers were forced to find jobs in other industries, leaving construction behind.

The economy improved. Construction projects resumed, and demand for workers far exceeded the available talent pool.

Nearly a decade later, owners in the construction industry still struggle. Many feel they are just one or two key hires away from the elusive financial and life freedom they dreamed about when starting their business. Again, maybe you can relate.

I knew I could help. The majority of our clients are contractors and are successfully solving their hiring challenges with my system. The Hire the Best System™ works in this industry. Not only are clients solving their hiring challenges, but they are creating highly profitable great places to work. As of this writing, some are taking 4 week vacations!

To write this book, I started with the core principles that work successfully over and over again. I conducted independent research as well as interviews with my clients, other successful construction business owners, and leaders in the industry.

With this research, I updated, expanded, and adapted the system I outlined in the first edition of *How To Hire the Best* to address the unique challenges and opportunities for contractors.

What you hold in your hands is that updated, expanded, and adapted system. It is specifically designed to help you find, hire, and keep the best team members.

The strategies in this Contractor's Edition of *How To Hire the Best* will help you finally take control of your business and life to unlock the full benefits of business ownership. Who knows, your 4 week vacation may be closer than you realize.

As you dive in, I want to help you attract top performers right away.

I know you're fed up and ready for solutions. That's why I've created a companion resource for this book: the **Hire the Best Toolkit™** to get you on your way to building your A-team—you know, your team of reliable, get 'er done go-getters. Are you ready?

Get access to the **Hire the Best Toolkit™** here:

www.TapThePotential.com/Toolkit[1]

---

1 - To make it easy for you to access all the resources mentioned in the book, plus get access to the Toolkit, I created a webpage just for the Contractor's Edition in the *How To Hire the Best*™ Series. You can access that here: *www.TapThePotential.com/Toolkit*. In addition, I have a coaching company, Tap the Potential, where my team and I coach entrepreneurs in applying these strategies and more to transform their businesses into highly profitable great places to work. Many then go on to join our 4 Week Vacation™ Program where we help them finally break free from the day-to-day demands of their business. Hiring the Best is core to all we support business owners in achieving.

Chapter 1

The #1 Challenge and the Tap the Potential Solution™

"Bad companies are destroyed by crisis. Good companies survive them. Great companies are improved by them."
—Andy Grove, former CEO of Intel

You are in an enviable position when compared to many businesses. While some businesses struggle to find work, those in construction often don't have that problem. The opportunity is big. Yet, that creates its own set of problems.

The bounceback following the housing crisis, low interest rates, a roaring stock market, and several other factors have generated plenty of construction and renovation projects.

The impact is incredible, too. Empty lots become family homes. Larger lots become neighborhoods. Unused or underused rooms transform into places where memories are made. New life and energy come to communities. The impact lasts for generations. You are creating legacies.

We change the way people live in their homes, and that changes their lives. They talk about how they hated their kitchen before, how they never had people over. But when we're done, they talk about how they have a gorgeous space to entertain family and friends. They're living a better life because of the space we create or recreate for them.

—Diane Hatfield, Hatfield Builders and Remodelers, Plano, Texas

Construction has a place in my heart. I like constructing things. I like the sound and the feeling of when things are getting built. I like the human aspect of it. This isn't just, 'We're slapping up some molding or building an addition.' This is a family that maybe they're expecting a baby or their kids are growing up there, and there's all of this transition, or they're retired or whatever the case is. It's a very people-oriented business. A lot of it is about bricks and sticks, and building it, but at the same time, there's a lot more to it.

—Mike Bruno, Stone Creek Builders, Matawan, New Jersey

We're more than just a home-improvement company. We're actually a brand that's woven into the fabric of our community. We make a difference not just in the lives of people inside our company, but also in the lives of individuals inside of our community.

—Brian Gottlieb, Tundraland, Kaukauna, Wisconsin

So much potential, but how do you tap into it?

The construction industry had its share of challenges before the recession and burst of the housing bubble in the late 2000s. Those challenges pale in comparison to the challenges of the current skills gap. The American Society for Training and Development defines a skills gap as "the point at which an organization can no longer grow or remain competitive because it cannot fill critical jobs with employees who have the right knowledge, skills, and abilities." This is the challenge many in the industry are facing.

How did we get here?

Between 1959 and 2007, housing units started *never dipped below 1 million during a full calendar year. According to the U.S. Census Bureau, the number of privately owned housing units started rose steadily from over 1.5 million units in 2000 to more than 2 million units in 2005. In 2006, housing starts dropped slightly, to 1.8 million units. In 2007, the number dropped to approximately 1.35 million units.*[2]

Then 2008 hit . . .

Between 2008 and 2013, housing units started never hit the 1 million mark during a single year:

- In 2008, only 905,500 units started.
- In 2009, housing starts bottomed out at 554,000 units.
- In 2010, housing starts increased slightly to 586,900 units.
- In 2011, housing starts increased slightly again to 608,800 units.
- In 2012, housing starts increased to 780,600 units.
- In 2013, housing starts inched closer to the 1 million mark, reaching 924,900 units—four years after the Great Recession officially ended.[3]

To put these numbers in perspective, the total units started in 2005 was greater than the total number of units started in 2008, 2009, and 2010 combined. From the 2005 peak to the 2009 valley, housing starts decreased by more than 70%.

While we still haven't come close to the pre-recession number, housing starts climbed steadily to approximately 1.25 million units in 2018.

Housing starts are only part of the story. The impact of the Great Recession reached far beyond new housing starts. Remodeling spending dropped. Consumer lending froze. Home values plummeted, leaving homeowners with little to no equity to borrow against even if they *could* qualify for a loan.

Nonresidential construction spending plummeted, too. After peaking at more than $34 trillion in 2008, total private construction spending for nonresidential projects dropped by more than $12 trillion in 2011 according to the data from the U.S. Census Bureau.[4]

Construction and remodeling—residential and nonresidential—essentially collapsed.

---

2 - *https://www.census.gov/construction/nrc/pdf/startsan.pdf*

3 - *https://www.nber.org/cycles/*

4 - *https://fred.stlouisfed.org/graph/?g=mxaA*

How the Great Recession Impacted the Construction Job Market on the Way Down

As demand plummeted, many companies were forced to close. Those that stayed in business slashed their workforce to meet the lower demand. They cut their prices to secure what few jobs remained.

The U.S. Bureau of Labor Statistics reports that the construction industry lost nearly 2.3 million jobs between 2006 and 2011. Many of those workers never came back, even when construction work rebounded. In fact, economists Hubert Janicki and Erika McEntarfer report that 60% of displaced construction workers left the labor market or moved into other industries. Only 40% stayed in construction.

The lengthy recession also deterred younger people from entering the industry in the first place. It makes sense, of course, given what was going on with the economy and the prominent role the construction industry found itself in. Why would anyone pursue an industry in crisis?

In fact, skilled-labor jobs were all in crisis during that time, not just construction jobs. But with fewer young people pursuing a career in construction, the workforce aged. In fact, a HomeAdvisor survey found 78% of skilled laborers are between the ages of 35 and 64.[5] Researchers say the trend is due to younger workers having a negative view of the industry and being pushed toward college degrees. A report by CBS Sunday Morning notes 70% of graduating high school seniors head to college. On average college graduates leave school with $37,000 in student loans.[6] Add to that the opportunity cost of not working while pursuing a two or four-year degree, and the cost rises further. Instead of working and earning money, they are studying and spending money.

Another report issued by the Washington State Auditor finds a similar

---

5 - Cusato, Marianne. "The Skilled Labor Shortage: Where is the Next Generation of Craftsmen?" *HomeAdvisor.* February, 2016.

6 - To view the report, visit *https://youtu.be/DcNGxALpVx0.*

28

trend of students being steered to bachelor's degrees instead of skilled-labor jobs.[7]

These reports paint a frustrating picture for finding skilled labor. Tens of thousands of dollars in student debt can be crippling. It can severely limit their ability to choose a career path based on their talents and passions. They have bills to pay.

The effect of this time-and-money commitment on the construction industry cannot be understated. The reaction for a college student is naturally to pursue a career in their area of studies. They will feel this push for years, even if they realize the career is not a good fit for them after all. While many will transition away from their area of studies over time, it might take years to make that transition. The rationale is not wanting to "waste" the time and money spent getting the degree.

Once they do commit to transition away from the sunk cost of pursuing a career that was not a good fit, it is too late for many of them to "start over" and pursue a career in construction. They earn too much money by that point and cannot afford to take a step back to a lower salary.

These studies reinforce the idea that construction companies should help the next generation pursue construction-related education opportunities straight out of high school.

The National Association of Home Builders (NAHB) in 2016 asked 2,001 young adults between the ages of 18 and 25 what they wanted to do for a living. Of the 74% who said they knew what they wanted to do for a living, *only 3% said they wanted to go into the construction trades.*[8]

In late 2017, Aaron West, CEO of Nevada Builders Alliance noted that 24% of the construction-related workforce is over age 55 and only 7% are under age 24.[9] This alarming trend is called the "gray tsunami."

7 - McCarthy, Pat. "Leading Practices for the State's Secondary Career and Technical Education Programs" *Office of the Washington State Auditor.* December 19, 2017.

8 - *http://www.nahbclassic.org/fileUpload_details.aspx?contentTypeID=3&contentID=255983&subContentID=694485&channelID=311* | *https://www.cnbc.com/2017/10/31/desperate-for-workers-a-colorado-homebuilder-starts-a-free-school.html*

9 - *https://www.recordcourier.com/news/business/construction-worker-shortage-seen-as-scary/*

According to data sourced by CBS, at one point, for every skilled worker entering the workforce, there were five retiring.[10]

Together, the lack of work, layoffs, bad press, and emphasis on college education has left the construction industry with an aging workforce.

But that does not mean all hope is lost. The recent focus on how crippling student loan debt is puts a new focus on the actual value of a college education. According to the National Center for Education Statistics (NCES), the number of students projected to attend American colleges and universities has fallen from a peak of 21 million in 2010 to just below 20 million.[11] The NCES projects annual attendance to remain below 20.5 million people each year between now and 2027, the last year of its projections.

Demand Rebounds—and How You Can Find Help to Keep up With Growing Demand

As demand for construction rebounds and continues to strengthen, construction companies face more and newer challenges.

Growing demand is a welcome trend after the meltdown experienced during the Great Recession. Companies still haven't built enough of a workforce to keep up with the rising demand.

These *new hiring challenges are frustrating. Many are still stinging from the heartache of laying off trusted workers during the Great Recession. Many are still digging themselves out of debt and near financial ruin. All the while, your ticket to stability and growth is right in front of you.*

Yet it continues to be just out of reach because you don't have access to the labor to meet that demand. In fact, 93% of participants in a HomeAdvisor survey said they believed their business would grow over the

---

10 - *https://www.cbsnews.com/news/labor-shortage-a-new-blueprint-for-americas-construction-trades/*
11 - *https://nces.ed.gov/fastfacts/display.asp?id=372*

following year if not for hiring challenges.[12]

Imagine that. Nearly 100% of companies say hiring challenges are keeping their business from growing. This effect is being experienced all across the country. In December 2017, the executive vice president of the Building Industry Association of Central Kentucky, described the construction industry labor market as "dire" in an interview with the *Lexington Herald Leader*, summing up what he's seeing as follows:

> *We desperately need more folks in the skilled trades. After the downturn in the economy of the housing market, so many of our skilled trade workers left the industry and didn't come back. That's left a huge void, not only here in Central Kentucky, but across the country that any construction company, anyone wanting work done in any type of building is facing right now.* [13]

To add to the problem, according to the Bureau of Labor Statistics, the number of construction jobs is projected to grow by 11% from 2016 to 2026, *faster than the average for all occupations.* [14] The U.S. Department of Labor estimated that 11.5 million jobs will need to be filled between 2016 and 2026.[15] According to the Bureau of Labor Statistics, the overall unemployment rate in the U.S. has trended down ever since hitting a peak of 10% in October 2008, even hitting historical lows of less than 4% in late 2018.[16] This is a welcome trend for the employment pool, of course. It also means fewer people are in the market for a new job at any given time. A proactive and creative approach to hiring is needed more than ever.

12 - Cusato, Marianne. "The Skilled Labor Shortage: Where is the Next Generation of Crafts-men?" *HomeAdvisor.* February, 2016.

13 - *http://www.kentucky.com/news/business/article190224014.html*

14 - *https://www.bls.gov/ooh/construction-and-extraction/home.htm*

15 - *https://www.bls.gov/news.release/pdf/ecopro.pdf*

16 - *https://data.bls.gov/timeseries/lns14000000*

Solve Your Hiring Challenges to Tap Your Full Profit Potential

Difficulty finding the right people with the right skills is the number-one reason entrepreneurs in the construction industry struggle to take advantage of growth opportunities. The cost of missing out on growth opportunities is difficult to measure, and who wants to? Thinking about what you might have made in the last few years if you doubled or tripled your profit is depressing.

Growth opportunities are the reason you are in business! When you fail to take advantage of opportunities, you set off a vicious downward spiral of too much work, too high stress, and too little profit.

You need strategies and systems. This book is on overcoming your hiring challenges with cutting-edge business strategy and The Tap the Potential Solution™ to growing a highly profitable, great place to work, even in the tightest of labor markets. Many of our clients are using it to grow their businesses with A-Players.

I'll also introduce you to some of our clients. They are entrepreneurs in the construction industry across the country, who are solving their hiring challenges. I'll share strategies and insights from industry leaders, whom I've had the honor of interviewing about challenges and opportunities they're seeing in the industry.

Mark Richardson is an author, Senior Industry Fellow at the Harvard University Joint Center for Housing Studies, and co-chairman of Case Design/Remodel and Case Handyman Services. He shares insights about the future of the construction industry, emphasizing that companies can't solve their labor shortage by bringing on more warm bodies. I couldn't agree more!

Companies must adapt their operations to reduce their need for more people. They can become more productive with fewer and sometimes different types of employees. He emphasizes how important it is for businesses in the construction industry to get creative. The opportunity lies in innovating to get more done without necessarily needing more people to do it. This will be the future of the construction industry.

It may seem ironic coming from a small business hiring expert, but here is a piece of brutal truth I tell every one of my clients:

> **If you can get away without hiring, you absolutely should.**

When I share that truth with clients, they sometimes ask if I am suggesting they continue to work too hard for too little money. That could not be further from the truth. In fact, if you accept my advice as truth and build your team with that in mind, you can make *much* more and work *much* less. The secret is building lean but mighty teams. This creates several cascading advantages:

- A smaller payroll while top-performing team members are well compensated
- More profit
- A better workplace culture, which makes it easier to attract and retain A-Players
- The greatest benefit of all is greater growth potential when you are less dependent on labor that may or may not be there.

As frustrating as labor challenges are, there is hope. Challenges bring the opportunity to innovate. You *can* achieve the growth you've worked so hard to have at your fingertips. Creative hiring strategies and ways to reduce your dependency on labor will help.

By the end of the book, you'll have the best strategies I've developed, tested, and shared with thousands of entrepreneurs.

The Tap the Potential Solution™

The solution to your hiring challenges will come through effective execution of these five strategies:

1. Design Your Business to be Sustainably Profitable

Yes, I know, it's tempting to have a fleet of new trucks with your logo, a fancy sign, a lot of employees, and millions in revenue coming in. Those are symbols of success. Or are they?

When I was a girl, my parents scrimped and saved to send me to private school. They dropped me off every day in our old pickup truck, or worse, our powder blue Oldsmobile Cutlass Supreme. My friends nicknamed it "the boat" when it became my first car. Every day, I cringed in the drop-off line as my peers were dropped off in sleek, brand-new Mercedes and BMWs. They wore shirts with alligators on them. When I told my mother I needed one of those, she got me a shirt with a dragon on it. Close enough, right? Wrong! I complained loudly at the dinner table about my parents' "shortcomings" with respect to their choices in vehicles and clothing. That's when I learned a life lesson that has stuck with me to this day.

You see, my father was a banker. Most of his customers were small business owners, and they were in debt. He informed me it is possible to drive a BMW and wear alligator shirts while you are drowning in debt. In fact, he alluded to many of my peers' parents being his customers, some of whom struggled month after month to make their payments. My parents chose vehicles and clothing we could pay for without going into debt.

Now, I admit, at that time, I still didn't understand the full implications of "being in debt." It wasn't until I completed my PhD and started making payments on my student loans that I got it. Debt is crushing. Debt kept me awake at night worrying about how to pay the bills month after month. I quickly found a creative solution to paying off my student loans, which I'll share with you later in the book. For now, I'll share that life has a way of coming full circle.

These are conversations my co-host, Mike Bruno, and I have on the *Profit by Design* podcast every week (*www.ProfitByDesignPodcast.com*). Success is not about how many trucks you have, or how nice your sign is (although Mike will tell you he was really proud of his sign). Success is about designing a business to be sustainably profitable so that you can live the lifestyle you desire.

> ## "Work supports life . . . not the other way around."

It's not about the money you make. It's about the money you keep. It's about the money that is in your bank account. It's about your business giving you a comfortable lifestyle as an entrepreneur so that you reap the rewards of all your hard work and the entrepreneurial risk you bear. After all, if you're working long hours to make payroll, you're working too hard for someone else's paycheck.

As Dave Sullivan, host of the *Roofer Show* podcast says, "I don't want to be the biggest guy in town. I want to be the most profitable." He's got it right. Let me explain.

Of small businesses in the United States, 85% are paycheck-to-paycheck businesses. This means they are barely breaking even, year after year.[17] The owners of these businesses essentially own their job. That job comes with a heck of a lot of headaches and responsibilities. If there is no profit, what is the point of owning your job?

> ## Design your business to be sustainably profitable.

Profit is the return you earn on your entrepreneurial investment. If you invested in the stock market and earned a 1% return on your investment, you'd be ticked, right? If you earned a 3% return on your investment, now you're doing a little better, but you're not even keeping up with inflation. So, why would you want to own your job to earn 1–3% profit year after year, or worse, come up negative. And, as I am sure you have experienced, if you are at 1–3% profit some years, there are some years you are

---

17 - Michalowicz, Mike. Profit First: *A Simple System to Transform Any Business from a Cash-Eating Monster to a Money-Making Machine. Portfolio, 2017.*

negative. There's just not enough margin with 1–3% profit.

It's time to think differently. Design your business to be sustainably profitable. Make strategic decisions based on profitability.

Take your profit first. This is what we help our clients do through my coaching and consulting company (*www.TapThePotential.com*), a Profit First Mastery Firm. Many of our clients are enjoying profit of 10% to 15% or more, year after year. Now that's what I call a good investment. You can do this, too!

Trust me, I've handheld many a business owner through this. I know what's on the other side for you, and it's pretty darn good. You probably won't have as many trucks on the road, and your sign won't be as fancy. But, I'm betting you'll be okay with that, right? After all, you'll be sleeping at night and taking vacations while your business grows in your absence. Sound good? Okay, onward.

> "Do not go where the path may lead, go instead where there is no path and leave a trail."
> —Ralph Waldo Emerson

2. Niche Down with a Clearly Defined Sweet Spot

Have a clear niche. Become the sought-out solution in that niche. A tightly focused niche broadens your opportunity for scalable growth, while streamlining your business, reducing your labor needs, and driving profitability.

Complexity is the enemy! Standardized repeatable work makes it much easier to systemize, automate, and scale a business. All of this translates into greater profitability for you (along with fewer employee headaches).

> **"Complexity is the enemy!"**

Mark Richardson is very direct about pursuing a simple niche business model. As he describes it, "If the business is focused on bath remodeling, the learning curves of bath remodeling versus full service design-build are very different from each other." He continues, "The more that you can bring someone on to focus on a niche of types of projects, the learning curve is shorter; you can see returns more quickly."

The benefits of niching down are immediate and important. You can do more and better work with a smaller, specialized team that does not need constant supervision. You have fewer people to pay, so you can pay your specialists higher wages, while lowering your overall labor costs and increasing profit.

At the same time, **with the cost of labor rising, you have to charge more to cover your labor costs.** Many of our clients come to us struggling to be profitable. This is due to the compound effect of years of undercharging in an attempt to remain competitive. Being the specialist within a clearly defined niche allows you to be competitive and charge what you need to charge to be profitable.

> **Being the specialist within a clearly defined niche allows you to be competitive and charge what you need to be profitable.**

You can justify pricing higher when your company is the specialist. In *Surge*, Mike Michalowicz shares the following analogy. When you get sick, you go to the doctor. If you have a cold, you're fine with seeing a general practitioner. But, if you're having chest pain, you want to see a cardiologist, and you're willing to pay the higher fee.

You will be able to command higher fees for your work when you are the specialist. In fact, in Mike's research of physicians, he's ascertained general practitioners command only 1/10 the fees specialists are paid. Let that sink in. The riches are in the niches!

At Tap the Potential, we help our clients become the specialists by zeroing in on the sweet spot of the business. The sweet spot is the intersection between your top clients' needs, your company's strengths (what you do exceptionally well day in and day out) and unique offering, and the systems in place to deliver that service (see image 1). This process is based on the book, *The Pumpkin Plan*, by Mike Michalowicz.

Let me be very clear. This is a process that is even more refined than simply identifying a niche for your business. The process of Pumpkin Planning your business laser focuses on your greatest opportunity to be sustainably profitable within a well-defined niche.

As the first strategist to become certified in the Pumpkin Plan, I've had the privilege of a front-row seat to witnessing the impact of well-executed Pumpkin Plans in our clients' businesses. Business owners who go through this process with us fall back in love with their business. A business with a clear sweet spot is much more profitable, easier to manage, and you get to work with your favorite clients. It also makes hiring much easier. What's not to love?

3. Innovate

Niching down makes it easier to innovate within your niche. Innovate with technology and automation as well as building materials and processes that reduce your need for labor.

Innovate to Remove Labor Inefficiencies

Mark Richardson says most construction businesses could further reduce labor needs by 10 or 20% by cutting inefficiencies. Most inefficiencies relate to the amount of labor involved. If three people are on a project, three people will work on a project. This is Parkinson's Law in action. Parkinson's Law states that work expands to fill the time available to complete it. When it comes to project-based work, work expands to the time and people allotted to do it.

Reflect on your own experience. Think about the last time a warm body quit. You probably saw your A-Players hunker down and pick up the slack, all the while sighing with relief that the warm body was no longer around.

Early in my career, one of my clients kept stalling on the strategic work we needed to do to get his business in order. Week after week, he'd tell me

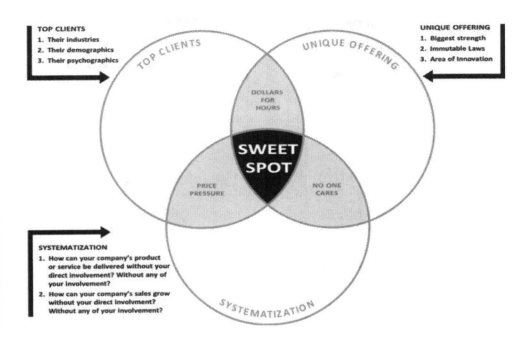

Image 1. Michalowicz, Mike. *The Pumpkin Plan: A Simple Strategy to Grow a Remarkable Business in Any Field*. New York: Portfolio/Penguin, 2012, and Pumpkin Plan Your Biz (*PumpkinPlan-YourBiz.com*)

"We're shorthanded, so we need to hold off on some of these higher-level initiatives until we get that solved." One day, I challenged him: "Shorthanded is the new *status quo*. Let's design your business around the assumption that you will always be shorthanded." He was finally able to move forward.

Restrictions forge creativity and innovation. Being shorthanded is the new *status quo*. Design your business with that in mind. It's time to get creative and innovate.

> **Being shorthanded is the new *status quo*. Design your business with that in mind. Get creative and innovate.**

Other inefficiencies have to do with inconsistent or inefficient process-es. To cut down labor needs—and costs—look at your processes. Look at the tasks you and your team do on a regular basis. Have you documented best practices and trained your team on performing them? If not, document your preferred way for performing these tasks, and train your team members to follow that process. Better yet, tap into your most efficient team member's process and have that team member train the others.

If you do have processes in place, evaluate them. What steps can be eliminated? What inefficiencies can you remove? Approaching it with a mind-set of improving efficiencies instantly reduces your labor needs—and costs.

Mark gave an example of a small remodeling project needing 200 la-bor hours. Implementing best practices and training your team members to perform efficiently might reduce labor hours by 20%, from 200 to 160. You deliver the same product to your customer. You might even charge the same fee if you bid on the project as a fixed fee. But your labor costs just reduced by forty hours. That is now profit! If you do that on one project, you can do it on another. When your labor needs are reduced across the board, you are improving your profitability significantly.

As you can see from the example above, hiring more help may not be the best solution. In fact, that can undermine your profitability quickly! Hiring the best team members to work within an efficient system *is* the solu-tion. Examining processes and implementing best practices forces you to eval-uate how you and your team are spending your time.

> Hiring more help may not be the solution. Hiring the best team members to work within an efficient system *is* the solution.

Get Creative in How You Use the Team You Have

Can team members use their skills to complete tasks in hard-to-fill positions? Can supervisors do a little bit of the labor functions while waiting for inspections? If you go into the analysis determined to cut down labor needs by 20%, efficiencies often appear. There are a lot of creative ways you can strip out some of the labor needs.

Identify Niche-Specific Efficiencies

Once your team is used to your leaner and more efficient model, repeat the process. Identify more or new inefficiencies. For example, Mark notes remodelers typically determine the products used to complete jobs. Many people think the homeowner does, but the remodeler guides even if the homeowner makes the ultimate choice. It is simple to lead homeowners to products that help them achieve their vision but need less work.

Consider replacement windows. One type of window with a certain kind of nail flange might take forty-five minutes longer to install than another. The homeowner wants a window. They want a certain look. They want energy efficiency. They want a quality window. But most would readily select a window choice you recommend if it satisfies their goals.

Evaluate the products you use, and train your team to recommend quality products that take less time to install. Your clients still get quality products. Your team members get simpler products to install. And you reduce your labor needs and costs. Everyone wins.

Innovate Using Technology

Before hiring, a critical question to ask is this: How can we use technology and automation to reduce the need for labor? Mark shares an example of System Pavers, an outdoor-living company investing in robots to install pavers. The robots can install pavers five times as fast as a person. This one technological investment allows them to do significantly more work in less time. Don't be misled. This company invests heavily in their team development, too. They automate work that does not need a human being. They reallocate the resources to growing their people, which makes it easier for them to attract A-Players. I'll be sharing more detail about that with you later in the book.

Robots installing pavers is just one example of new technologies to help you do more with your existing team, or even reduce the size of your team. Another benefit is increased accuracy. Robots also come without drama. As The Business Psychologist™, I regularly have business owners confiding in me that they are "done with the drama." The lack of drama is the biggest benefit of robotics!

I imagine you might be thinking, "Wow. That's very expensive to invest in something like that." But contrast that with payroll—typically the biggest expense in business. Imagine investing in robotics to cut costs of wages, benefits, supervision, sick days or other time off, and inconsistent work. Reducing the cost by even one team member would be significant. Additionally, you will be able to bid on more jobs knowing you will be able to perform the projects. You will be able to raise your prices because your clients can be more comfortable the work will be performed well and on time.

Robotics become an investment to consider when you have a clearly defined niche and strong demand for your service.

Beyond robotics, there are other ways to get more efficiency from your team using technology and automation. Christeen Era of Core Growth Strategies suggests using timekeeping systems and software. They streamline operations and reduce payroll inefficiencies. Adding time-tracking software can save you between 2% and 8% on payroll costs by increasing accuracy and ease of timekeeping. With GPS timekeeping, your team members' hours will be tracked automatically. It can make you more money by ensuring your team members stay on job sites as long as they are expected to be. Projects get completed sooner, which allows you to complete even more projects.

4. Build a Lean and Mighty Team

No matter how much you niche or innovate to reduce labor needs, you will need *some* team members to run your business and perform tasks. If you cut your needs down by 20%, make sure whoever is on your team is the *best available*. This means you will have to be realistic about what you pay for labor, and price appropriately. Too many small business owners are eating the costs of labor, and it's driving their profit down while driving them out of business.

Time and again, in our clients' businesses, we see that one A-Player can do the work of nine to twelve "warm bodies." Not two. Not five. Nine to twelve. A-Players are more engaged and more productive. They make fewer mistakes. They come to work on time. They work even better when they do not have to correct problems created by "warm body" coworkers. When you identify their strengths and deliberately align their strengths with the results you need from them, watch out. They will blow you away with what they can do!

Successfully growing your team comes down to this: Hire top talents who are good fits for clearly defined roles. Compensate them well. Create a great place for them to work that retains and attracts A-Players. The efficiencies and profit growth you gain through niching and innovation make it much easier to do that.

> ## The Tap the Potential Solution™ for Growing Your Team and Your Profit:
> Hire top talents who are good fits for clearly defined roles.
> Compensate them well.
> Create a great place for them to work that retains and attracts A-Players.

A great culture reduces your need to hire because you will be *retaining* talent. A great culture also makes your business highly desirable for A-Players. A great culture makes people work hard and support each other to find and use efficiencies.

A great culture creates a true team environment where everyone looks out for each other and your business. You become an "employer of choice" with a pipeline of highly qualified candidates eager to join your team.

If you like the idea of building a great culture that attracts A-Players and are struggling to make this a reality in your business, our team is here to help! This is what we specialize in. Our Exclusive Small Group Coaching Program supports you in being the leader you need to be to create a highly profitable, great place to work. You can learn more and apply at *www.TapThePotential.com*.

5. Network using the Hire the Best A-Player Attraction System™

While A-Players are everywhere, they are hardly ever actively looking for work. They are employed. So, you must always be on the lookout for A-Players and build relationships with them. If you wait for an opening, you are too late.

Always be recruiting.

Use strategic networking to develop a steady pipeline of interested candidates for your next opening. Get my How To Hire the Best Toolkit™ (*TapThePotential.com/Toolkit*) to dive into this right away. This is a critical system to get in place in your business. The sooner the better!

Start Now

I have many tools to share with you to reduce labor needs, increase profit, and improve performance through innovative hiring. To help you get started, I created a video tutorial at *www.TapThePotential.com/Toolkit*.

The Tap the Potential Solution™ to Scaling a Highly Profitable Business, Even in the Tightest of Labor Markets

1. Design Your Business to be Sustainably Profitable

Focus on growing profit over growing revenue. It's not about what you make. It's about what you keep. Take your profit first.

2. Niche Down with a Clearly Defined Sweet Spot

Complexity is the enemy. Create a clear niche around your sweet spot. Become the sought-out solution in that niche. That allows you to systemize and automate some things, decreasing your time and labor needs.

3. Innovate

Innovate with technology, automation, building materials, and processes that reduce your need for labor.

4. Build a Lean and Mighty Team

Design your business to operate with a smaller team. Invest in that team by hiring top talent for clearly defined roles. Compensate them well, and create a great place for them to work. Work on yourself to be the leader you need to be to create a highly profitable, great place to work.

5. Network Using the Hire the Best A-Player Attraction System™

Always be on the lookout for A-Players, and build relationships with them. If you wait for an opening to start looking, you are too late.

What's Possible...

Perhaps you've believed your business' growth potential is being throttled because you haven't been able to hire the team you need. I invite you to set that belief aside.

Just imagine . . .

What would life be like if you could make simple tweaks to *how* you do business to tap into your full *profit* potential?

What would it be like to actually *increase* production with fewer team members?

What would be possible if you could attract and hire the best team members for your company?

What would be possible for you if all of these things were true?

Keep reading . . .

Chapter 2
The Impact of the Labor Shortage

The shortage of labor presents four specific challenges for you as a business owner:

1. Finding exceptional team members
2. Hiring exceptional team members who fit with your culture
3. Tolerating team member disengagement
4. Firing too slowly

Challenge #1: Finding Exceptional Team Members

According to the Associated General Contractors of America, 80% of construction companies nationwide have trouble finding qualified team members.[18] This is harder when companies are not just seeking *qualified* team members but *exceptional* ones.

> **A-Players are rarely unemployed and looking for work.**

Consider that any population consists of about 10% A-Players. This means 90% of the people you encounter are B-, C-, D-, or F-Players. Furthermore, *A-Players are rarely unemployed, reading job ads, and looking*

---

18 - *https://www.ecmweb.com/construction/80-contractors-report-difficulty-finding-qualified-craft-workers-hire*

for work. They probably work elsewhere. A-Players typically move from one opportunity to the next. This explains why utilizing standard hiring practices typically results in mis-hiring. The odds really are stacked against you until you find better strategies for finding and hiring top team members.

Your attraction and hiring strategies need to align with how A-Players move from one opportunity to the next. **Typical hiring strategies are out of alignment with the behavior of A-Players.** What I'll be teaching you aligns with A-Player behavior, and it will make your hiring process much more effective.

Because the challenge of finding exceptional team members seems difficult, you may feel as if you have no choice but to lower your standards. By lowering standards, you end up building a team of marginal members. They need excessive management, create problems with work ethic and quality, and bring others down. You might as well be spraying A-Player repellant all over your business.

Time and time again, owners who lower their hiring standards confide in me they spend way too much time managing team member problems. Some even say they long to simplify their business and go back to the days before they even had team members.

It doesn't have to be this way.

Chad Hatfield of Hatfield Builders & Remodelers emphasizes how important it is for him and his wife, Diane, to find exceptional team players who share their personal and company values. He also shared how difficult it can be sometimes.

> *My main role and functions in the company include sales, making sure that everything is running the way that it's supposed to, and hiring the right people. Everything that we do here is about people. It's incredibly personalized, so relationships are the most valuable thing to each of us. That's sometimes hard to find in people.*

Mike Bruno of Stone Creek Builders focuses on not just finding qualified team members but exceptional ones. Mike formed Stone Creek Builders in 2004, after doing home improvement projects around his neighborhood since 1992. After growing his business to nearly thirty team members, he was forced to cut back significantly when the economy turned south.

Mike coped with marginal team members while struggling to find exceptional ones. After experiencing how much work—and stress—it created to settle for marginal employees, Mike decided he would be more patient and intentional when hiring, even subcontracting out some work until he found truly exceptional candidates. In his words,

> *We self-perform some of the work, we subcontract some, we have office staff, but it's been a huge flux in terms of how many employees we have, expanding, contracting, expanding, contracting. Over the last five to ten years, it's just become increasingly more difficult to find even good qualified people, which then makes you just think about the business a little different . . .*

Spending too much time dealing with marginal to poor team members can have a lasting negative impact on you. Some owners sour on the idea of growing with team members and end up working too hard for too little money, essentially going from owning a business to owning a job. They go back to a one-person show, doing all the selling, work, paperwork, and billing. When they don't work, they don't make money. That means no vacations, no growth, and sometimes no hope.

> "When I let go of who I am, I become what I might be."
> —Lao Tzu

The lack of quality team members can send you down the slippery slope of self-doubt questioning your own ability to lead. When I hear an owner questioning his or her ability to lead, the first questions I ask are about the quality of the team members the owner is trying to lead. Many times, the issue is the quality of the employee more so than the quality of the leader.

When you tolerate mediocre team members, work quality suffers, and you spend too much time managing the mediocre team members.

Mike points out, "As the business owner, you have to take full responsibility for everything, and there's no excuse beyond yourself. I also don't think we're responsible for the accountability of the employee, but these people have not been trained or educated in a 25- or 30-year career on how to act as a team member working for a construction business in a small business environment."

This is an important point to consider. Our educational system is not preparing students to be active problem-solving, collaborative team members in a fast-paced, rapid-growth, small business environment. Furthermore, team members who come to you from other businesses have not been trained in how to be an effective team member.[19]

When you are managing too many warm bodies, things spiral quickly. You and your better team members work too much because you are managing poor team members and cleaning up behind their mistakes. You have less time to sell. You have less time to put systems in place to make things run more smoothly, so mistakes continue. When poor team members leave, you may rush to replace them with the next warm body because you're overwhelmed and can't imagine having to do even more work. The cycle repeats itself as the business spirals downward.

Mike uses the metaphor of "runny eggs" to explain why it is not a good idea to spend time and money on team members who are marginal to poor.

> *After learning these Hire the Best™ strategies for the first time in my career, I'm looking to fill those positions only if the person is right. In the past, it's always been, 'We need this person. Who cares? We have to get them on the job because that's what we need to do.'*

---

19 - This is the very reason I created Leadership Bootcamp at Tap the Potential. In six weeks' time, we are equipping our clients' A-Players with the skills and strategies they need to be an effective team member in our clients' rapidly growing businesses. You can learn more at *www.TapThePotential.com/Leadership*.

If you have twenty guys running around like maniacs, and you hire another, even if he's an A-Player, you mix him with a bunch of C- or B-Players, the whole thing's a mess.

The reality is, if you go out for breakfast with your family, and all the eggs come out runny, and everything's a disaster, you're not going to go back the next time.

Yet, how many employers continue to write a paycheck every single week to a team member who is not performing to the standards? They're getting runny eggs every single day, and they're doing that because they feel like they can't eliminate that person and they need the body there.

That's also a very difficult thing to do, because traditionally, I was always a very emotional business owner in terms of, 'I hired this person. I feel bad. I don't want to let them go,' that kind of thing.

I've contracted the size of the business, and I'm willing for it to take the time that it takes. The way that I look at it at this point is that paying team members is no different than any other experience that I'm paying for.

The good news is if you use the techniques I am sharing with you to attract exceptional team members, you won't need as many team members. One A-Player can do the work of nine to twelve C- and D-Players. With innovation, creativity, and a system for adding great team members, your business can stabilize. Then you will be more profitable with fewer team members.

This is especially true in the construction industry. I will show you how to effectively reverse the mediocre team member cycle through innovation, creativity, and recruitment of better candidates. Our clients increase revenue with *fewer team members. They achieve even greater profitability and create a thriving culture that attracts exceptional candidates.*

Powerful Questions to Drive Innovative Solutions to Your Labor Shortage

Payroll is the biggest expense in a small business. Complexity is the biggest threat to the sustainability of your small business.

People are complex. The more your business relies on labor performed by people, the more layers of vulnerability you are adding to your business. Instead, focus on hiring a few great team members. Compensate them well, and reduce your labor needs.

That is the Tap the Potential Solution™ for a highly profitable, great place to work.

Before adding new team members, ask yourself the following questions:

- Why are we even doing this job?
- How might we do this job differently?
- How might we outsource it or drop it all together?
- How might we divide the job up among several of the people already on staff?
- How might we use technology or automation to do the job? (e.g., voice mail and direct-dial numbers have replaced duties of a receptionist.)

Challenge #2: Hiring Exceptional Team Members Who Fit With Your Culture

When you do find that exceptional candidate, you may feel a lot of pressure to "sell" him or her to work for you. That can have several negative consequences. You might fail to screen and interview appropriately because you are so focused on convincing the candidate to come to work for you. Instead of hiring a candidate who is a good fit for the position, you end up hiring based on who was most convinced they want the job. When business owners hire a candidate whom they have "sold," the employee is in a "one-up" position and may expect the owner to meet demands going forward.

Brendan and Mandy Wilkes run Cabinet Depot in Pensacola, Florida. Avoiding the tendency to "sell the position" to candidates has changed their hiring process.

Brendan and Mandy now focus only on hiring exceptional team members. One of the big benefits of this shift in focus was improving their confidence turning away people who are not good fits. As Mandy describes it, it's critical to "make sure we really know who we are as a business and thread that into that job posting to push away the people we don't like and attract the people we do, that we are like-minded with."

I worked with Brendan and Mandy to develop a job posting that reflected who they were while simultaneously helping separate exceptional candidates from mediocre ones. Instead of posting a "vanilla" job ad that listed job duties and experience or education requirements, Brendan and Mandy got creative, working their company culture into the job posting.

Below is a copy of the job posting. As you'll see, Brendan and Mandy were very up front about what life would be like for the candidate if they were hired. They also showed their personality in the wording they used.

Finally, they included two challenges to candidates to test them. First, they intentionally included some grammar "issues" and offered "bonus points" to candidates who spotted them. Attention to detail is a critical trait to succeed in this job. Second, after letting candidates know part of their responsibilities would be to greet customers in the showroom as needed, they asked candidates to visit their website, learn more about their company, and figure out who they would be replacing if greeting customers were their main job.

They asked candidates to place the name of that team member in the email subject line when they delivered their resume and references, as "_____'s replacement." This invites the candidate to learn more about their company and their team by visiting their website. Only a candidate who is truly interested after reading the job advertisement will take the time to do that. Here's their ad:

Are you a multi-tasking ninja? Are details your jam? Do you do puzzles for fun?

We are offering a Full-Time job to someone who finds organization thrilling, who loves a fast-paced day, who finds juggling a breeze, likes people, and doesn't need us to babysit you.

Working with us won't be your boring run of the mill corporate job. We are a family run, small business and that is how we like it. We want to know all about your family, what your dog's name is, what you did last weekend, your favorite movie of all time. None of us here have won the lottery yet, so if we have to come to work, we want to spend our time with people that want to work hard and play hard. So if you don't play well with others, no need to continue reading.

We are a sales-oriented team. But what we are selling is more than just cabinets or remodeling. It is an experience. We take every opportunity to help people in every way we can. Because of this, you have to have passion for what you do. You have to want to do your job so hard!

You will be dealing with people. All the people. All the time. The sales team, the warehouse guy, the customers, the subcontractors, the vendors, the mailman, the order taker at our favorite wing place. All those people come fully stocked as real humans, not computerized. So if you find you are allergic to dealing with different personality types, this job will definitely give you hives.

We don't take someone spending their time or money with us lightly. We consider it an honor. So you have to be on board with making sure that we are doing what we said we would do, when we said we would do it, the way we said we would do it. Every little detail matters and there are SO MANY DETAILS in the work we do. Because of this, you have to be a master of the universe when it comes to details. You also have to be able to think through all those details, and organize them like your job depends on it.... No really, you can't have the job if you aren't a detailed and organized person. Being analytical and observant is what is going to set you apart from the rest. We LOVE problem solvers! Not problem identifiers. Anyone can point out the elephant in the room, but how do you move that big beast out of the way?

You will also need to feel comfortable leading team meetings. This isn't a public speaking job. We just want you to be able to communicate effectively with the team the specifics of open projects and give direction where needed.

We are like peacocks around here. We are so proud of the work we do! We find joy in seeing our hard work come to fruition and seeing our customers get the kitchen or bath of their dreams. No one has shackled anyone to a desk around here. We are here because we want to be here and we love what we do. If you want to work with a family full of peacocks, you should do the following.

Send us your resume. Make sure to include at least 3 professional references because we check 'em! Part of the job is to greet customers in the showroom as needed. We would like for you to go to our website, learn more about our company, snoop around and figure out who you would be replacing if that were your main job. Place the name of the team member in the email subject line as "_____'s replacement".

Once you do this, we will reply and send over the boring, factual job description. If you are still interested after reading the job description we send to you, reply back in the subject line, "Hey! I want this job!". Then tell us in the email why you think you would be a super good fit with our team. Also, brownie points for anyone who checks this ad for errors in grammar or punctuation.

Cheers!

The ad was a success. While they got dozens of applicants, only four followed all the directions and emailed their resume and references with the right subject line. The fact that only four applicants followed the directions is what makes this a success. This process saves you valuable time wading through resumes and applications. If an applicant shows you right away they can't follow directions, they have saved you a lot of money because you did *not* hire them in the first place. Mis-hiring and turnover are two of the biggest hidden profit suckers in small business. Avoid these and build profit.

Remember, an applicant can have great qualifications but may not be an exceptional fit for your culture. It is much better to find this out during the application and interview than after you have hired the employee and spent time and money on training. The traditional hiring process provides limited information. Assessing goodness of fit based on it is challenging. Large corporations have entire Human Resource Departments charged with recruiting and hiring. You're doing this on your own, while wearing many hats in the business. People are complex. Most small business owners don't come into business with a doctorate in psychology. You need better tools and strategies to increase your success with hiring. I want to equip you with these tools and strategies. I teach these in depth in my course at *www.TapThePotential.com/Course*.

Ronda Conger, Vice President of CBH Homes in Meridian, Idaho, understands that exceptional team members are not just people who can perform high-quality work. They are people who are a good fit for the culture of your office. CBH Homes operates with a tremendously productive and loyal team. What's more impressive than what they do and how productive they are is how they achieve that productivity:

> *Love wins! I feel like that's what has driven me my whole life. I decided a long time ago that love beat every other emotion. It beat fear, or anger, meanness, jealousy, all those other ones. I felt like when you love who you are, you love your company, you love your team, I always say, you love your buyers. You're going to win, right?. . . If you're the leader of any company or anything, what you believe in and how you operate is going to affect all those around you. I think that's why it's even*

more important that I firmly believe that love should be at the basis in my opinion.

Ronda's team is succeeding. Not only is her team incredibly productive, but theirs was named one of Idaho's Best Places to Work in 2017.[20] I'll share more of Ronda's strategies with you later in the book when we focus on creating a great place to work filled with loyal team members.

The Costs of Hiring the Wrong Person

Traditional hiring practices are posting an ad, collecting resumes, interviewing, and checking references. The typical business owner using those practices will mis-hire 75% of the time.[21]

Mis-hiring is costly and time-consuming. An analysis by Inc. Magazine referenced data estimating the cost to replace an $8 per hour hourly employee to be $3,500.[22]

There are many different formulas people use to calculate costs. Most estimates project the cost of a bad hire to be two to three times the person's salary. According to Harvard Business Review, costs of employee turnover range between 100% and 300% of the replaced employee's salary.[23] In other words, mishiring a supervisor that makes $20,000 per year will cost you between $20,000 and $60,000. Hire the wrong $100,000 per-year manager, and you could be out between $100,000 and $300,000. Add to this a decrease in morale, business, and satisfied customers. Pile on the cost of recruiting and training a new employee, and you've got every business owner's nightmare.

20 - *https://www.bestplacestoworkinidaho.com/companies/1190/year/12/profile*

21 - Smart, Bradford D. *Topgrading: The Proven Hiring and Promoting Method That Turbocharges Company Performance* (3rd Edition). New York: Portfolio/Penguin, 2012.

22 - *https://www.inc.com/the-build-network/turnover-costs.html*

23 - *https://hbr.org/2015/03/technology-can-save-onboarding-from-itself*

> "As a small business, what do we want to eat? Do we want to eat fast food, or do we want to eat vegetables and healthy food? Do we want to surround ourselves with positive, energetic people, or are we just looking for quick wins? Are we looking for great salespeople regardless of culture and fit, or are we looking for people that believe in our mission because we clearly identified it, and we're going to grow a sustainable business model?
>
> It's very tempting for a new business to go after quick wins, when in fact, it's not a sustainable growth model."
> —Brian Gottlieb, Tundraland

Filling positions with warm bodies is like going after quick wins—only worse because you lose both in the short and long term. You might staff a project this week but likely cost your business much more in the long term.

Challenge #3: Tolerating Employee Disengagement

"The company is our people."
—Gary Kelly, CEO of Southwest Airlines

Business owners often tolerate a lot of "bad" employee behavior just to keep some team members around to get some things done. See if this sounds familiar:

You know you're not getting the best out of these team members. They don't go the extra mile for your customers, even though you've had "that talk" repeatedly in staff meetings. Their morale is low, they show up late, leave early, and stand around chit-chatting when you can see twenty things they could be doing. The truth is, they do just enough to get by. Plus, they often make mistakes that cost you lots of money in rework.

If you are like most owners, you watch your bottom line closely. **Payroll is typically one of the largest expenses.** Although *payroll* is an expense in our financial statements, the team members behind that payroll are assets. They are responsible for leading your company into the future. Whether they are productive or not, they will determine your future. The better you invest in them, the better your future will be.

With that in mind, compare your mindset on team building with your mindset on investing in new equipment or a stock in your investment portfolio. Do you research equipment before buying it? If you choose a lower-quality piece of equipment, do you blame the equipment when it breaks down, or do you try to make a better choice next time?

What about stocks in your investment portfolio? Do you just pick any stock, or do you try to find quality ones you believe will give you the best return, even if it costs more per share than other stocks?

Team members are not an expense. They are an investment. You invest payroll, leadership, training, and other time and money into your team. You also invest in your team members by listening to them and continuing to invest in improving the tools, systems, and processes you provide to support your team, even when times are tough.

Investing what you can to support your A-Players at all times helps you build deep relationships with them. Don't turn your back on them when things go south. When things are better, they will still remember that you did not have their backs. That will make them just loyal enough to stay until they find a better offer. If you expect your team to be accountable to you in good times and bad, you need to be accountable to them as well.

Hiring team members is an investment, and it's up to us as business owners to make sure that investment is worth it. If we hire the right person, they're an investment that's worth it. If we hire the wrong person, they are an expense, costing us time and money. The better you become at investing in the right team members and developing them, the more productive and engaged they will be and the better your return on investment will be. If you don't, your payroll can also be the source of a significant hidden profit bleed—employee disengagement.

> "Life shrinks or expands in proportion to one's courage."
> —Anais Nin

The Cost of Employee Disengagement and Ineffectiveness

For the typical construction business, the cost of employee disengagement can range from several hundred thousand dollars to millions of dollars—*annually*. Just imagine . . . what could you do with that money if it were profit?

We tolerate marginal team members because we think we need to . . . to survive. But, in actuality, this is the slow kiss of death for your business.

> **Your payroll can also be the source of a significant hidden profit bleed: employee disengagement.**

Unhappy, disengaged team members spend only 40% of their time on task.[24] They may show up to work five days per week, but you only get two days of work out of them.

---

24 - Pryce-Jones, Jessica. "Positive profits: How happiness at work impacts the bottom-line." *Choice*, Volume 11, Number 4, pp 27-28.

The price of keeping disengaged, ineffective team members is high. Most of us have no idea how high.

Lost productivity costs the U.S. economy $588 billion a year. A national study by Dale Carnegie Training placed the number of "fully engaged" team members at 29%, meaning nearly three-quarters of team members are not fully engaged.[25]

Most companies have as much as 85% of their human resources doing just enough to get by and sometimes even less. The average employee is discontented, underutilized, and not actualizing their potential. They also are less likely to be happy, healthy, satisfied, and fulfilled.

The costs from team member disengagement can mount quickly in a construction business. As just one example of the impact disengagement has, consider what happens when a disengaged team member installs a product incorrectly. There are costs for replacing damaged materials, plus extra labor hours spent correcting the problem. You likely will have a frustrated client because the project is delayed. If you are already shorthanded, this delayed project spills over and causes delays with other projects. That results in other costs and places additional pressures on team members, impacting morale.

You don't have to tolerate disengagement when you have a system for attracting A-Players to your team *and* the skills to create a great culture.

The Engagement Matrix

Taking an inventory of your present human resources can help you see where you are losing money.

---

25 - *http://www.dalecarnegie.com/imap/white_papers/employee_engagement_white_paper/*

The Four Quadrants of Engagement & Effectiveness[26]

Team members generally fall into one of four categories regarding their level of engagement and effectiveness. These can be represented in quadrants as labeled:

Engaged & Ineffective (EI)	Engaged & Effective (EE)
Disengaged & Effective (DE)	Disengaged & Ineffective (DI)

The Engaged & Ineffective Quadrant (EI)

New hires typically fall into this quadrant. New team members are excited and engaged but usually ineffective. When new team members come on board, they have a lot to learn before they become effective. New team members are learning their way around the office, who reports to whom, and your day-to-day operations.

New team members generally are excited and motivated to do their best work for you. They just don't know *how* to do so. New team members are also a great source of new ideas and can give you feedback to improve your current systems. However, they typically don't have the depth of understanding of your industry and your systems to determine the most relevant feedback or ideas to share and/or implement.

Mike Bruno points out that not only does the new team member come

26 - Kienast, MCC, CPCC, Theresa A. "Engage Employees and Become a Superhero!" *Choice*, Vol 10, Number 2.

in excited, the business owner experiences "new-employee-hired euphoria," which is a dangerous place to be because it can lead to a lot of work being done improperly, or not at all. Here's how he describes it:

> *Now you have the new-employee-hired euphoria, where they come and they start on the first day, and you're like, 'This is fantastic. All my problems are going to be solved. This person's going to do all these things that I don't want to do anymore that need to get done for the business . . .' Now you start completely diluting why you hired them to begin with, and you go through the motions and you end up, six months later or a year later with a complete tangled mess, because every reason why you hired that person from the beginning, those things aren't getting done. Now you morphed them into something else that maybe they're not so good at.*

If instead, you navigate the new hire phase well with effective onboarding, all that excitement and energy continue into the next quadrant, "Engaged & Effective (EE)," where energy and innovation really come alive.

The Engaged & Effective (EE) Quadrant

Engaged and effective team members are still excited—and they have been around long enough to have a good working sense of the mechanics of the organization. These team members show up with powerful ideas and have the energy to move them forward.

They contribute with discretionary effort that no company could afford to pay for. They surpass expectations and want to create and implement their ideas.

It is ideal to have the majority of your team members in this quadrant. This is where you get high productivity with minimal mistakes. Much leadership training focuses on how to move team members into this quadrant and keep them there.

The Disengaged & Effective (DE) Quadrant

These team members often remain effective enough to get by, but their energy and creativity are gone. The danger of keeping them around is that they can start dragging others from the EE quadrant down with them as they become less engaged and effective.

I should also give you a word of caution here . . . many owners have an unarticulated expectation that as they learn, grow, and try new things, their long-term team members will come along for the ride. When the owner starts making changes for the better, we actually see turnover in long-term team members. They are *not* along for the ride. They liked the *status quo*.

"Cleaning house" can be a good thing but particularly stressful for business owners. They do not expect to lose long-term team members as they add in more accountability. I often tell clients, "Buckle your seat belt. This is a bumpy ride, *and* you will be better for it in the end."

Team members who start out engaged but then become disengaged may be coachable, but you need to intervene with them early. Many business owners procrastinate. They hope the employee's lapses are temporary and the employee will eventually re-engage. Don't delay! Address issues as they arise.[27] Employee disengagement feeds on itself. Negativity begets more negativity. Discouragement leads to more discouragement.

The Disengaged & Ineffective (DI) Quadrant

Disengaged and ineffective team members complain, have low morale, repeatedly make mistakes, and might even sabotage company efforts. Despite this, very few will do enough to actually get fired.

Instead, they continue to drain energy and suck the life out of other team members and the company as a whole. These team members will cost you a bundle and can sink your business. Let them go!

---

27 - If you need to bolster your skills in addressing disengagement, you are not alone. I designed the Coach Approach course to help leaders like you have these crucial conversations with their team members. Learn more at *www.TapThePotential.com/Coach-Approach*.

For a tool to calculate the hard costs of employee disengagement in your business, go to *www.TapThePotential.com/Toolkit*.

Six Primary Reasons for Employee Disengagement

Why does disengagement happen?

Most experts blame immediate supervisors for employee disengagement. Certainly, a bad boss who yells and belittles team members will lead team members to become ticked off, apathetic, and disengaged. However, in my experience, most of the owners with whom we work are not bad bosses. In fact, they care considerably for their team members and yet they still have problems with disengaged team members. Here are the six primary reasons for employee disengagement.

1. Team Members Not Understanding Their Role in the Story of Serving Your "Ideal Client"

FACT: Most business owners don't have a compelling story about the "why" of their business and how their business serves a need of their ideal client and customer, much less a story that is appealing to their ideal team member.

When team members buy into why your business exists, why you are passionate about the customers and clients you serve, and why what the employee does matters, they are much more likely to be engaged. Taking out the trash is no longer just a chore to be done. It becomes a part of the whole story about why what you do matters.

Brian Gottlieb's team members at Tundraland understand the role the company plays in their clients' lives. In his words:

We're a home improvement company, and we do baths and windows and walk-in baths and decks and such. But that's only what we do, that's not really who we are. Products in an organization come and go.

If you would've asked me what the business was at the time I started, I would've said, 'Well, we're in the construction business.' If you ask me today, I would say, first and foremost, 'We're a training and development organization.' And that's really what we do. It's about teaching and developing others to accomplish something greater than they ever thought possible before.

Give Your Team Members a Story Worth Telling

Brian Gottlieb founded Tundraland right in the midst of the Great Recession. In less than ten years, he took Tundraland from operating on a plastic folding table with $3,000 cash to a company employing nearly 100 people and doing more than $18 million in business a year. His secret, as he describes it, is creating and protecting a great company culture.

Brian gives every employee a "story worth telling:"

My leadership style tends to be inspirational. I share with people the vision of where we're going and create small attainable goals along the way that are definitely stretch goals, but create attainable goals that people can achieve so they start to buy into the bigger picture. I find it to be effective to put out a very, very, very big, aggressive goal that's inspirational and creates a story worth telling.

For example, even today, every single new division of our business begins on a plastic folding table, like Tundraland started back in 2009. We do that not just as a matter of driving sales revenue, keeping costs low, and all that other stuff you want to do when growing a business. ***It's about making sure you're always providing an environment that gives every single employee a story worth telling.*** *Bringing people along on a journey as a startup company and constantly making it special for them along the way is so important.*

To help you give *your* team members a story worth telling, here are a few questions to get you started:

- Why do you do what you do for your best clients or customers?
- What are the greatest, most important problems you solve for your best clients or customers?
- What impact does solving those problems have on your best clients and customers?

Go First and Encourage Others

"On May 6, 1954, probably one of the most important and significant sports records of all time was set. What made that record so significant was not that it would never be broken. Nowadays, records are set all the time. But we all believe that, one day, somebody else is going to break it. It doesn't matter what record it is. Records are meant to be broken.

What happened on May 6, 1954, nobody believed could ever even happen. It used to be thought impossible. People thought the human body was incapable of doing it. People thought it was literally impossible.

It was the day that Roger Bannister ran a four-minute mile. Before Roger Bannister, the mile record had stood for years because people thought it was humanly impossible. Once people saw Roger Bannister break four minutes and survive, all of a sudden, the impossible became possible.

Within three months, thirty-five more people ran a four-minute mile—something nobody had done...until Roger Bannister did it.

Today, there's nothing special about a four-minute mile in professional racing. But it represents the idea somebody has to go first. Somebody had to believe in something that was so crazy for themselves and then accomplish that and encourage others to then do the same.

That is at the core of Tundraland's business model. We help others realize and achieve their own four-minute mile. We help people believe in something even if everybody else around them, even if they're surrounded by people saying, 'You're never going to do that.' Well, of course, they're never going to do that because it's not their four-minute mile!

That's how to bring a brand to a community. How do we go big, bold, and like nobody else could ever do? How do we have our own four-minute mile and believe, not by being limited based on anything, but instead, believing in being limitless?

We go first and encourage others."

—Brian Gottlieb, Tundraland

Take the time to create your compelling story about why you do what you do for those you serve. Then, make your team members heroes in the story! Tell the story every chance you get, starting with the initial employment interview, and continuing on from there.

Your team members need to know their hero role. Most don't. We all like to be heroes. Give your team members the chance to be a hero, and watch them do their best for your customers!

There are lots of opportunities to make your team members the heroes. Visit *www.TapThePotential.com/Toolkit* to access an exclusive bonus clinic to help you turn your Immutable Laws into compelling stories that engage your team members.

Let's look at the next reason your team members become disengaged. This one is pervasive!

2. Letting Too Many Slackers Hang on for Too Long

Letting too many slackers hang on for too long drags down morale. Your best people get tired of cleaning up messes made by the slackers. Plus, word gets out. Exceptional team members do not want to work with a bunch of warm bodies. By keeping warm bodies around, you are actually repelling exceptional team members.

In the words of Mike Bruno:

> *Don't keep any warm bodies. Get the emotions out of it. You have a responsibility to your clients, to your family, to your business, to be productive. Employees have a responsibility to be productive for you. If they're not, you can't make excuses, you gotta cut them loose and go on to the next one.*

Allowing slackers to hang on too long leads to the third underlying cause for team members becoming disengaged.

3. The Boss Exhibiting Bad Behaviors

(Notice, I did not say "bad bosses.")

Managing team members who constantly make mistakes and who do just enough to get by is maddening for even the most patient of bosses. We all have our breaking points.

Mike Bruno struggled to be patient with team members, especially when they made mistakes. He was repeatedly frustrated by the drama that arises when he criticized someone for not executing on the work he needed finished. Drama simply does not coincide with his personality type. Perhaps you relate:

> *I slightly joke around about it . . . but I say I hate employees. It's not that I hate employees or I hate people. I like people. What I dislike is the complacency that develops, the drama, and it doesn't blend well with my personality type. So, I've learned that my personality type, I'm not a soft-people-skills type of person; I'm a let's-get-to-work person, how-come-it's-not-done person.*

Mike shares his insight on how he deals with this in Episode 7, "The Emotional Side of Managing Employees" on the *Profit by Design* podcast.

You can find a link to this podcast in the Toolkit at *www.TapThePotential.com/ Toolkit.*

When bosses lose their patience with bad employee behaviors, at the worst, the boss yells and screams. That not only ticks off the employee he or she is yelling at, but word gets out, and morale goes down for everyone. You feel guilty. Your guilt eats at you and makes you even grumpier. It's a vicious cycle.

Long before you lose your cool, something more insidious happens. It's our human nature to notice and focus on problems. Once you see one problem, you see more and more. It becomes much more difficult to acknowledge what your team is doing right. You become a boss "on patrol," continually noticing and commenting on mistakes and oversights, feeling like you are always lecturing your team about what they are doing wrong.

A good rule of thumb is to strive for a *7:1 ratio of positive to negative comments to your team members.* When you get out of balance by focusing more on the problems, rather than what your team is doing right, morale goes down, and even the best team members will become disengaged.

Mike's story about understanding how his personality type matters is something that might help you, too. One of the greatest impacts we make with business owners through our Exclusive Small Group Coaching Program at Tap the Potential is helping them understand their personality type and how it impacts their team. Understanding your personality as a leader is key to becoming the leader you need to be to have the team you want to have.

Your personality type influences who you should choose for your team. Most of us try to hire people like us. That's the wrong approach. We need to build teams with complementary personality types and learn how to tap into our team members' strengths to get the work done. It's also important to understand how personality type relates to job duties required of each position. A more in-depth discussion on the role of personality in hiring is available in the accompanying course at *www.TapThePotential.com/Course.*

With that understanding, owners can find people who are more likely to both get along with them and have the right personality for the duties they will need to perform. For example, if you're like many in the industry, you may be blunt and to the point. Maybe you're known for losing your temper quickly. If that's you, it's a good idea to hire people who are not overly sensitive, who don't hold grudges or stew over things. You need people around you who can take offense, tell you they're offended, and get over it quickly so everyone can get back to work.

It also means you will need to be prepared to have people on your team who are blunt as well. You can certainly learn soft people skills over time. But, let's be honest. That's never going to be a strength if your natural personality is to be blunt. There is value in learning soft people skills. It's much more effective to embrace your natural personality, though. Then find team members who fit well with it. I also want to be clear that I am not suggesting you hire team members who are just like you. You need diversity on your team for it to function effectively. What I am suggesting is that you be mindful of your nature as you hire team members.

Mike has experienced success with this approach, too. Be more mindful of personality types when hiring and do not worry as much about soft people skills. Mike says, "We can escalate a conversation and have a little bit of emotion in there, but then we're moving to the next thing very quickly, as opposed to somebody who you say something to, their feelings get hurt, they walk away, and then nothing gets done."

4. Failing to Delegate

As much as we business owners want to delegate, we can fail miserably in our execution of this. Failing to delegate will drag down morale. This often occurs because we do not trust the team members we've hired to get the job done.

When you have disengaged or ineffective team members, you don't delegate the $10/hour tasks, much less the $100/hour or the $1,000/hour tasks. You never get around to tapping the full profit potential of your business, where you get to do your *$10,000/hour work*.[28] Let's face it, if you—the CEO, the president, the owner—are not doing your genius work, your business is losing money daily.

---

28 - For more on this topic, listen to my webinar, "How to Make Your Time Worth $10,000 an Hour," available from the homepage at *www.TapThePotential.com*.

There is no reason for you to neglect your business by performing activities that do not play to your strengths. Most of us overestimate how well we perform various tasks. The mere fact that we wear many hats and have a long list of things to do means we are not executing any of our tasks at the highest level. Delegating, especially tasks others can do better, frees your time to focus on your strengths and prevents you from selling yourself short. Removing just one activity that is not your strength can make a major difference to your business and attitude not to mention your effectiveness.

Delegation creates the mental space you need to innovate and move your business forward. When you effectively delegate and spend the majority of your time doing your genius work from your strengths, you'll find you can work far less than 40 hours per week, while your business moves forward by leaps and bounds. In fact, after working with us a short time, some of our clients start scheduling their 4 week vacations. They are mastering effective delegation.

Effective delegation is key to keeping your team members engaged. Exceptional team members want to feel competent. Competence comes from being stretched to take on new responsibilities and master new challenges.

Don't hesitate to delegate, thinking you are somehow "protecting" a team member from becoming overwhelmed. Ask your team members to tell you if they are overwhelmed by the responsibilities they are being assigned. Then trust them to do so. If you have good communication with them, they will tell you when they are maxing out.

Delegate and support your team members in carrying out their responsibilities. You'll be amazed at what others can do, especially when you've aligned their duties with their strengths! Many of our owners experience great pride in watching their team members succeed.

Now, let's examine another reason team members become disengaged. This one is subtler, and many business owners overlook it.

5. A Mismatch Between the Team Member's Immutable Laws and Yours

Many new hires are excited to work for you. They start out engaged, even though they are relatively ineffective because they are still learning the ropes. Once they are trained and have been with you for a while, they are exactly the kind of employee you want—engaged *and* effective.

Yet some of those who start out excited then go on to learn the ropes and become top performers will become disengaged. This has nothing to do with anything you, the boss, has done to them. It's simply due to a conflict between the employee's Immutable Laws[29] and yours. Immutable Laws are your core values, your fundamental, deeply held beliefs, your highest priorities, and the organizing principles that guide your actions. This is why identifying your Immutable Laws early on is key to a successful hire.

Mandy and Brandon Wilkes of Cabinet Depot have experienced tremendous success in their business by making a few simple tweaks, including identifying their Immutable Laws and using them in their recruiting and management. Mandy explains that team members need to have an equal exchange of energy to offer. Equal exchanges of energy is an Immutable Law for Mandy and Brendan. If a team member doesn't share this Immutable Law, they're simply not the right fit for Cabinet Depot:

> *I've always lived by the theory, 'There has to be an equal exchange of energy' because in any relationship, whether it's a relationship with your spouse or with a friend or with a coworker or money or food or whatever it is, if it's unbalanced, it doesn't work.*

Mandy and Brendan have both experienced the power and freedom that come with finding matches between team members and company Immutable Laws. As Mandy puts it, "One of the things Dr. Sabrina has really helped us with is putting a structure around the hiring process so we're not just blindly putting job ads out in the market. It's really different than anything we've ever done before, and it's definitely a different mindset."

Surprisingly, the most damaging team members to keep around are top performers whose Immutable Laws are not aligned with yours. These team

---

29 - Michalowicz, Mike. *The Pumpkin Plan: A Simple Strategy to Grow a Remarkable Business in Any Field.* New York: Portfolio/Penguin, 2012.

members are poison to your business. Even though they perform well, they show a very different set of values from yours.

For most owners, this presents quite the dilemma. It's hard enough to find great team members. If you have a top performer who consistently handles situations in ways that make you cringe, you have a conflict based on Immutable Laws.

What should you do with them? Terminate them. They damage the integrity of your business in the eyes of your other team members and your customers. By keeping them around, you end up sending mixed, confusing messages that drive away your best team members and customers.

For example, your top salesperson brings in a lot of revenue but rolls his eyes at the new initiatives you introduce and state-of-the-art training you share in weekly meetings. Maybe he tells your customers that some of what you offer is "irrelevant" to their needs. Because of this, he never shares your latest value-adds with customers because he doesn't see the point. Although his sales make a significant contribution to your top-line revenue, he fails to bring in additional revenue because he is not leveraging all the tools and training at his disposal. Furthermore, he's a negative influence on other team members, one of whom recently confided in you that she has looked for work elsewhere because she is so troubled by the ongoing negativity coming from your top salesperson.

Although it may be tough to let this person go, in the long run you'll be glad you did. Most owners breathe a sigh of relief after letting a team member like this go—and their team members do, too!

> "You can choose courage, or you can choose comfort, but you cannot choose both!"
> —Brené Brown

Later, we'll take a deeper dive into identifying your Immutable Laws. Finally, let's examine the sixth reason for employee disengagement.

6. Failing to Intervene Quickly When a Good Employee Shows the First Sign of Disengagement

You have a good employee who typically performs well and makes you proud. One day you observe this employee doing something out of character. Intervene as quickly as possible.

Too often, owners are inclined to overlook the problem, hoping it will go away. It won't. Chances are, you're seeing the first sign of a more serious problem to develop. Address it quickly and hold the employee accountable for improvement.

Here's how to coach this:

- Get curious, in a nonjudgmental way, about what is going on with this employee.
- Express your surprise at this sudden change in the employee's behavior.
- Be curious about the underlying cause *and* what the employee will do to immediately turn it around.
- Ask how you might support the employee in efforts to turn the situation around.

Employee disengagement is costly to your bottom line. Take action to address these six underlying causes of employee disengagement and watch your team thrive.

What is a happy employee really worth?

Now that we've considered how much employee disengagement could be costing you, let's examine the value of a happy employee.

An extensive research program with over 32,000 participants conducted since 2005 by the iOpener Institute for People and Performance at Work concludes that happiness at work drives employee engagement.[30] **A happy**

---

30 - Pryce-Jones, Jessica. "Positive profits: How happiness at work impacts the bottom-line." *Choice*, Volume 11, Number 4, pp 27-28.

employee is a high-performing employee. Team members who are happiest at work:

- Use 1/10 the sick leave of their least happy peers
- Are six times more energized
- Express the intent to stay twice as long in their organizations
- Report being "on task" 80% of their work week, compared to their unhappy peers who report being "on task" a mere 40% of their work week.

Investing in solid strategy to maximize the number of team members in the Engaged and Effective quadrant is just sound business sense. Here are three immediate actions to take.

1. First, **systemize your onboarding and training to move your new hires** (i.e., your Engaged & Ineffective team members) to be effective as quickly as possible. If it currently takes you six months to bring a team member fully up to speed, what needs to happen to cut that time in half? And then cut it in half again? That's an opportunity to innovate. Remember, the time that is saved by becoming more efficient leads to more profit.[31]

2. Second, **set strong accountability expectations for each position** and let those disengaged, ineffective team members know about the accountability expectations. Track progress. They will likely look for work elsewhere soon. If not, encourage them to find work that is a better fit for them and let them go.

3. Third, **attempt coaching** with disengaged and effective team members. Keep in mind that not all of those team members will be coachable. If their Immutable Laws are not matched with yours, support them in moving on!

If there are other reasons for their disengagement, coach them in addressing those issues[32], set clear accountability expectations, and keep a tight time frame for change. If you do not see a significant improvement in their engagement within that time frame, let them go.

---

31 - To learn more about effective and rapid onboarding to drive engagement and loyalty, access our course at *www.TapThePotential.com/Onboarding*.

32 - If you need support in building your coaching skills, access our Coach Approach Course at *www.TapThePotential.com/Coach-Approach*.

Remember, letting one disengaged employee go creates the opportunity for you to hire your next top performer. This is what we call "hiring up!" It's a good thing for your team and your bottom line.

This leads right to the fourth challenge owners face due to the labor shortage.

Challenge #4: Firing Too Slowly

When it's so challenging to find good team members and get them to come to work for you, many owners fear firing subpar team members. In all the years I've been coaching and consulting, not one business owner has told me they regret firing a subpar employee, even if they don't replace the employee right away. In fact, they all say just the opposite. Often, it takes only one firing for a business owner to fire faster the next time around.

Keeping bad team members can have a host of negative consequences. These people can negatively affect other team members, create issues with clients and customers, cost you business, and even drive you to dislike coming to work at your own company!

Worse yet, keeping a bad employee around will get you questioning your judgment and leadership competence. Your negative self-talk is a slippery slope: *Why did I hire that employee in the first place? How did I miss the "red flags" in the interview? Why can't I coach this employee to be better? What's wrong with my leadership? Maybe I'm not cut out for this.*

Before starting Hatfield Builders & Remodelers, Chad Hatfield had worked in a $7 billion commercial construction company. At the time of the interview, he and his wife, Diane, have a team of fourteen people including themselves. Chad believes it's best to be honest with both yourself and a team member when deciding whether or not the job is working out. He makes clear that his belief is that the long-term consequences of keeping a bad employee are much worse than getting rid of the person immediately. To Chad. it is best to fire sooner rather than later.

We just got through really cleaning house . . . We let five people go between November and January, and we just said, "Anyone who doesn't meet the standard, we're through playing around with people. You're going to treat our clients and us in the business and its resources with the respect that it deserves, and we're going to have an ideal team." The long-term consequences of keeping them are always greater than the consequences of firing them now. And you are not doing them any favors either because if you feel that chances are they're not happy either, and it's just not going to work, and you're lying to yourself. So stop lying to yourself. Own up to the reality, give them honest feedback, and if it's not going to work, be honest with yourself with it, and find somebody else.

Once you hire someone, check in regularly to align expectations. Before you hire, ask yourself, 'How will I know this new team member is succeeding? What will success look like at the end of Day 1, Week 1, Month 1, 90 days, 6 months, and 1 year?' Be sure to communicate those expectations to your new team member, then check in regularly with a brief 1:1 meeting to align expectations.

Ronda Conger asks her managers to check in with new team members at regular intervals with the following questions:

Is it what you thought it was going to be? What's different? What didn't match?

As Ronda puts it, "maybe they say, 'I didn't know you worked so hard, I didn't know that I had to do this . . . You were the best place to work. I thought you'd drink beer all day.'"

Ronda also wants her managers to have specific, frank discussions about attitude and actions:

We need to have a really good feeling that you are showing the right attitude, the right actions, and we're going to get there. You're far from perfect, you're far from there but, boy, the attitudes and actions, those are the two things over the 90 days that we watch for. Are you excited? Are you ready? Are you grateful? Is your mind in the right place?

Are you doing everything that we ask you to do and then some? If you're not those two places, you're not going to be there past ninety days.

Ronda is very intentional about having her managers identify what new team members are doing great, what they need to stop doing completely, and what they need to focus on to get better.

In just fifteen minutes, managers can help new team members get or stay on track with their attitudes and performance.

Ronda also instructs her managers to ask what they can do better as a leader and manager. Her focus is to have the right people in the right spots. Having the same conversations with team members over and over again is not acceptable.

She has frequent, frank conversations up front but if something lingers after having been discussed, she gives team members thirty days to make the change or leave the company, saying something to the effect of the following:

It's obvious that you're not happy, you're not producing, you're not thriving. I only want people in the building that want to be in the building. People who are excited to be here, people who believe in the mission, and want to be here. If you don't want to be, please don't stay. You'll show me that based on your actions.

I want you to know that you will be just fine without that warm body employee. In fact, your business will be more profitable when you let that person go. Redistribute work among remaining team members, and operate with fewer team members as you attract the best team members to fill your open positions.

Ronda puts it this way:

I think sometimes we think, 'Oh, it's too hard to rehire. We'll make it work. We'll figure it out.' You won't. If they don't want to be there and they're not doing what you asked them to do, you have to be honest with yourself and with the person and say, 'You don't want to be here.'

81

Lessons in Letting Go, From Chad and Diane Hatfield

It's hard. It's real hard, and the people that know me closest, especially Diane, she had to deal with me every day, but you get to the point where you just, you just almost break down . . . You've got to keep going, and you need people to do that, but you've got to get rid of the cancer. You have to just cut it out . . . The long-term consequences of keeping them are always worse than the short-term consequences of cutting them out right now, and we just said to hell with it.

We're going to just make it, and if I can't find ideal people for this team, then it'll just be a smaller team and a smaller business because I'm not going to go through the crap that we've had to go through again, and have to have people not follow through, break stuff, hurt relationships with clients and damage jobs and not do things right, and then we have to stop what we're doing for people that care and dive in and rescue the jobs with herculean effort because we're going to make them right no matter what. I don't care what it costs, I don't care what we have to do.—Chad Hatfield

I think what we've experienced is that when we rid our environment of the negative people that were really distracting to all of us and were bringing everybody down... people rally together. Our team has rallied together and said, 'Okay, the Hatfields got rid of this person, so we're going to just make it work. What do I need to do? Tell me what role you want to step into, where can I help, where can I take over,' and they're digging in and diving in, and just getting after it, and they're staying late, they're doing whatever they have to do to make it work . . . I think the environment overall is better. Our team meetings are happier. The office just feels better. It just feels

> nicer when you walk in. Knowing that we're going to just move ahead and move forward keeps it positive and keeps it going, and we're not going to let all of these things that we had behind us and all these bad people that we had behind us drive us down."
> —Diane Hatfield

What's Possible . . .

If you've been holding on to subpar team members, what's possible if you let them go? What's possible for you? What's possible for your business?

Now, it's time to hire up!

Chapter 3
Attracting *Your* Ideal Team Members

Long gone are the days of having a team member quit, then running a classified ad to fill the position. Generic "help wanted" ads are almost useless for attracting good applicants. Remember, the majority of A-Players are employed elsewhere. They are not reading job advertisements daily. You need a different set of strategies to attract them.

First, acknowledge the urgency and importance of planning, networking, and recruiting to fill your open positions. This must become a strategic and ongoing focus in your business. Keep an eye toward creating a full pipeline of prospective, qualified applicants. This pipeline of qualified applicants will be your resource for future team members. Nurture your relationships with these people, understanding this is a long-term investment. Some but not all of your efforts will bear fruit and pay off over time with great candidates from which to fill your open positions. The importance of this strategic initiative is equal to the importance you place on business development.

> **Rule of Thumb**
>
> Once you have steady lead generation in your business, it's time to start networking to recruit for future open positions.

Where you find A-Players hinges on *when* you are looking for them. If you follow traditional hiring practices and post an ad when you realize you need help, you will be looking in all the wrong places to find A-Players. A-Players are hardly ever unemployed, reading job ads or postings on online job boards.

Furthermore, you can expect that about 10% of the population is composed of A-Players. Of those people, some will be children. Some will be elderly, and some will have a disability that prevents them from working. What's more, you can expect that almost *all* able-bodied A-Players desiring employment will be employed. This is why it is so hard to hire A-Players! But it's not impossible. It just takes some strategy and focused attention on your part. Remember, it's well worth your effort!

You need to "always be marketing" for your business to succeed. You also need to "always be recruiting" by networking with A-Players to grow a pool of applicants available for your future openings. The time to start this is *not* when you are desperate to hire. The time to start recruiting is long before you anticipate needing to hire.

Once you have steady lead generation in your business, you need to start networking to recruit for future open positions. Why? Because once you have predictable lead conversion, you will soon have a capacity problem. Once you have a capacity problem, *you* will be working 70+ hours per week *in* your business without a pipeline of A-Players who are interested in working for you.

Think ahead. What revenue growth are you anticipating in the next year? A 25% revenue growth annually will double your business in three years.[33] Some of our clients come to us desperate to hire because revenue growth has nearly doubled in the last year. Imagine the stress of trying to service that level of business, and not having the team you need. Now imagine the added stress of having to find time to learn and execute the best ways to attract and hire A-Players. Do you feel the pain yet? Good! I am simply trying to give you a clear vision of what's in your future if you don't get to work on building out your Hire the Best A-Player Attraction System™ *now*.

If you neglect to do this type of networking, when it's time to hire and you are drowning in more work than you can handle, you will be limited to the applicants who just happen to respond to your ads. Many of those

---

33 - Herold, Cameron. *Double Double: How to Double Your Revenue and Profit in 3 Years or Less.* Greenleaf Book Group LLC, 2011.

individuals will be unemployed—and there is a reason they are unemployed. That does not bode well for you.

You must come to grips with the time and effort that will be needed to adequately address this problem in your business. Recently, a business owner reached out to me due to challenges with finding and keeping team members. He told me this is an urgent and important problem, but he had very little time to devote to addressing it (*because he was so busy working in the business to cover for the shortage of team members!*). He wanted a "quick fix" and did not like hearing the harsh dose of reality I shared with him. His problem attracting ideal team members can be fixed, but not with just an hour or two of attention from him.

Business owners like you and I must get very smart about how we plan, network, and recruit to fill open positions. We must make attracting ideal team members a part of our strategic planning and keep it top-of-mind.

What's the word on the street about your business?

What do your team members say to their friends when they talk about work? When their friends complain about work, are your team members breathing a sigh of relief and bragging about how good they have it? Or, are they bemoaning the last thing one of their coworkers did that ticked them off? Or, worse yet, are they telling their friends about the latest thing their boss did to make their life miserable?

When it comes to attracting A-Players to work for you, having a great culture and a reputation as a great place to work makes it a lot easier. Yet, if we're being honest, most businesses do not meet these standards. In fact, the majority of businesses are not great places to work. Yet, many small business owners desire to have a great culture. Where's the breakdown? It's a combination of two factors:

1. The chaos that sets in when a business grows. Marginal systems get stretched to capacity and fail. This creates stress for not just you, but also for your best team members.

2. Insufficient team members to handle the demands placed on the business as it grows.

In the middle of all this sits a business owner who looks a lot like George in the image above. Maybe you can relate.

Remember what I said earlier about planning ahead for growth? As soon as you have steady lead generation in place, put attention toward recruiting team members. You will soon be experiencing growth. Intentionally work on your culture, and implement systems that will support a great culture.

The majority of our clients who enter our Exclusive Small Group Coaching Program are like George.[34] In fact, they've usually been feeling like George for quite some time before they find us. We help them navigate the challenges of being stretched beyond their and their teams' capacity, while creating a highly profitable, great place to work. So rest assured. Even though you may be stretched to your capacity now and it may feel nearly impossible to attract the team you need to go forward, there is a way out. We've helped many business owners get to the other side. I know what's on the other side of this for you, and it's pretty good.

Let me give you a glimpse of where we start . . .

---

34 - To learn more about our Small Group Coaching program visit *www.TapThePotential.com/Services*.

Crucial and Costly Mistakes Many Business Owners Make When Hiring

Mistake #1

Typically, owners make a decision to hire, advertise for applicants, and start the selection process without enough consideration for how the position serves the business' ideal client, how the position will be a profit center, and who the ideal candidate would be.

The next time you find yourself getting ready to hire, answer these questions:

- How does this position serve your ideal client (directly or indirectly)?
- In what ways can this position be turned into a profit center? (In other words, how can the person in this position make you money or save you more money than they cost you?)
- Imagine you have a top-performing employee in this position. What performance criteria will you hold that employee accountable to?

Mistake #2

Rather than defining who their ideal candidate would be for a position, they hire based on choosing who is best out of those who applied. If the pool of applicants is rather small, this limits the qualifications. So, rather than defining who is the perfect candidate for each position in their business, owners often let random people (job ad respondents) establish hiring criteria.

Instead of letting applicants and existing warm-body team members establish your ideal team member expectations, take time to envision and create your ideal team member descriptions.

When you know who your ideal team member is, identifying A-Players is easier. Now you know what you want. Creating job descriptions, writing advertisements for openings, and describing who you are seeking when networking will all be easier. Each step in your recruitment process will attract your ideal team members.

Before we taught Mandy Wilkes an effective way to find exceptional team members, the process was quite a mess. She posted on multiple platforms and was overwhelmed with results that were hard to narrow down. By learning how to post a more effective job ad, she was able to weed out the candidates who weren't exceptional team members. Here is how Mandy describes her experience:

> *We posted on Craigslist, and we posted on Indeed, and we posted it on Monster, and gosh, LinkedIn, lots of different . . . oh, Facebook. Lots of different places, and basically, we're flooded with every type of resumé from underqualified to extremely overqualified to someone that really didn't have any of the skillset we were looking to people that wouldn't really want this job. That takes an incredible amount of your day and life away because you're just sifting through these trying to figure out who in the world that you can call. It was just a painful process."*

Being clear about the person you are seeking to hire will save you countless hours of your valuable time.

What is an A-Player?

A-Players are your most valuable team members. These people have great attitudes. They always seek to work smarter. They take initiative and go the extra mile. These are the people you trust to get the job done. A-Players are good communicators who work as a team to accomplish goals.

A-Players contribute more than other team members.[35] **One A-Player typically does the equivalent of nine C-Players to twelve D-Players.**

---

35 - Smart, Bradford D. *Topgrading: The Proven Hiring and Promoting Method That Turbocharges Company Performance* (3rd Edition). New York: Portfolio/Penguin, 2012.

It's well worth the investment of your time and energy to attract more A-Players.

A-Players are resourceful and will get over, around, and through barriers to success. In fact, resourcefulness is the most important competency you should seek when hiring.

Keep in mind, none of these A-Player characteristics is "trainable." This is why it is much better to structure your process to attract people with these A-Player qualities. You'll have much more success training skillsets.

Here are some interview questions that can help you find out how resourceful an applicant is.

- When deciding how to organize your work, how do you assess what tasks need to be given priority?
- Share an example of not having the tools to do your job. How did you handle that situation?
- When was the last time that you tried a new idea to improve your work performance and what was it?
- If you were blamed for a mistake for which you were not responsible, how would you handle the situation?
- What would you do if you needed to make an immediate decision, but did not have the information you needed?

Resourcefulness is a defining characteristic to look for in A-Players. You need to go a couple of steps further in defining what an A-Player is for your business. You also need to consider the candidate's goodness of fit with your Immutable Laws or your non-negotiable standards. In addition, you need to consider the personality strengths needed to deliver the results of each role *exceptionally* well.

This requires some forethought before your next hire.

I'll walk you through this process. First, we start with clarifying your Immutable Laws.

Immutable Laws

What are your Immutable Laws? Immutable Laws are your core values, fundamental beliefs, highest priorities, and organizing principles that guide your actions.

The challenge most of us have is that our Immutable Laws are so much a part of the fabric of who we are that we have a hard time identifying them, much less putting them into written form to share publicly in our businesses.

We are happiest when operations in our business are in synch with our Immutable Laws. But, watch out . . . when one or more of our Immutable Laws is violated, we feel it. We get frustrated and angry.

Here's a Powerful Question for Identifying Your Immutable Laws:

What's ticked you off recently?

Think about something a team member, customer, or co-owner has done recently that really got under your skin. Chances are, one of your Immutable Laws was violated. Try to put words on the Immutable Law that was violated.

For example, one business owner shared with me that he was frustrated that his team members were showing up to work "around 8:00 a.m." and often were about five minutes late. He had repeated discussions with them about the importance of showing up on time for work. Things would get better for a few days, but then the team members would be right back to old behaviors, strolling in a minute late, then five minutes late, etc.

I asked this owner what "showing up on time" means to him. His reply was, "It means showing up five minutes early." Aha! This was an unspoken Immutable Law for him. Once he clarified this Immutable Law with his team members, his better team members began showing up early. If they were "late," they were arriving at 8:00 a.m. The owner was much happier with this pattern of behavior from his team members.

Take a few moments to brainstorm your Immutable Laws. Then, observe yourself over the coming weeks. When do you feel proud of your business? Chances are, an Immutable Law is being honored. When are you ticked off? Chances are, an Immutable Law is being violated. Capture these Immutable Laws, and add them to your list.

Mandy and Brendan were able to brainstorm their Immutable Laws together. They figured out what irked them and why they were irked. This helped them discover what unspoken Immutable Laws they abided by.

> *And so, we had to sit around the campfire and talk about problems that we had encountered and things that were super joyful. Because we didn't want all of our Immutable Laws to come from a negative place, because that's not really what it's about, right? It's who we are, all of us, all encompassing, not just the stuff that doesn't feel good. But we had to sit around and talk about it and we had to identify, "Man, when this happened, that sucked, and this is why. Why did it suck? What was the issue that made that . . . that made it hurt so bad?" Then we were able to really identify, get to the root of why. Why did that feel so bad? And that usually created the Immutable Law for us.*

Eventually, you will want to narrow your list of Immutable Laws. A shorter list is easily remembered by you, your team members, and your customers.

Narrowing your list and getting the wording right takes some time. So, start with brainstorming your list, then try it out for a while, making changes as you go.

Tap the Potential's Immutable Laws

Here are our Immutable Laws at Tap the Potential as examples to help you get started brainstorming yours:

We attract the best clients and serve the heck out of them! We devote ourselves to our clients achieving their highest goals and being their best selves.

Our clients can count on us. We do what we say we're going to do.

Walk the talk, even when it's hard. There's no other way. Be real. Take risks. Be vulnerable.

Being in business is tough . . . do the Happy Dance whenever you can! Celebrate wins, and intentionally do more of what works.

Mistakes are learning opportunities. Vent, learn, and keep moving forward! Giving up is not an option.

Work supports life . . . not the other way around.

Be a gift from our gifts. We seek opportunities to use our strengths to add value for our clients and our communities.

There are no "right or wrong" Immutable Laws. Create the ones that are right for you and your business. For more examples and support in clarifying your Immutable Laws, visit *www.TapThePotential.com/Toolkit.*

Chuck Parmely's Immutable Laws

Here is an example of my client, Chuck Parmely's Immutable Laws he created for his company, Overhead Door Company, located in Riverton, Wyoming:

Do it once, and do it right.

Say what you will do, and do what you say.

Do more than what is expected, under promise and over deliver.

Communication is a must; share ideas and concerns at all

> levels, field, office, and especially the customer.
> Provide exceptional customer service.
> Do an honest day's work for an honest day's pay.

Only hire people whose Immutable Laws are well-matched with yours. Pass up the applicant with the glowing resume if you don't feel like they get what you are about and what you are up to in your business.

Weed out team members who don't hold your Immutable Laws. It doesn't mean they are bad people. They just don't have the same core values as you. Over time, you'll have a leaner, higher-functioning team that you'll be proud of!

> **Team members who share your Immutable Laws are much more likely to stick around and be loyal to your company. They will be proud to work for you. They will have your back. Isn't that what we all want from our teams?**

Create Ideal Team Member Descriptions for Each Position

Ideally, you'll want to define the ideal team member for each position in your company. It takes time, and you are busy. So, keep it simple. Start with the position you intend to hire for next. Then, each time you have an open position, work through this process. Soon you will have clear descriptions of the ideal team member for each role in your organizational chart.

As you develop your description of your ideal team member for a position, ask yourself:

- What are the results I am seeking from a team member in this position? How will I know they are doing a good job?
- What personality strengths are needed to do this job exceptionally well?
- How will a team member in this position display our Immutable Laws?

Some ideal qualities, such as Immutable Laws, will be universal for every employee, while others will be exclusive to the position. For instance, punctuality and a good attitude are characteristics you no doubt want in every employee. Being great with numbers and able to spot mistakes are desired qualities in bookkeepers but may not be as important in a customer service role.

Using what you identified by answering the questions above, write a one-paragraph description of your ideal team member for an open position.

Chad Hatfield knows what he wants for a team member. He tests candidates with three characteristics. He creates the job description with clear intentions and expects the candidate to meet his expectations. Otherwise, they aren't the ideal team player he's looking for:

> *The ideal team player has to have three common characteristics. They have to be humble, hungry, and smart. They have to have humility, they have to be hungry to do whatever it takes to get the job done, and they have to be emotionally intelligent.*

Example: Project Manager Position

This person is a good communicator who is a detail-oriented, out-of-the-box problem-solver. They flexibly adapt to changes while managing many projects on deadlines. This person values looking ahead and taking a proactive approach to head off problems. He or she maintains a professional demeanor even under stress.

With a clear personality description like this, anyone with whom you are talking may be able to picture someone they know who is like this.

A word of caution: As you describe your ideal team member for the position, stick to personality descriptors. Avoid language that could be discriminatory. For example, using the word "energetic" may imply age discrimination if an older applicant has been turned down for the job.[36] Instead, you might describe the person you are seeking as a "motivated go-getter," which can apply to a person of any age.

Now let's take this one step further to position you to *attract* your ideal team member for your current opening.

What would attract your ideal team member?

Define why your business is a great fit for your ideal team member. Answer your ideal team member's unspoken question of "What's in it for me?"
- What is important to your ideal team member?
- How does your ideal team member stand to benefit from working for you?
- What is your Unique Employment Proposition (UEP)? In other words, what makes you uniquely suited to be a great employer for your ideal team member?
- What do you offer that your competitors don't?

Brainstorm a list of the top five reasons an A-Player would want to come to work for you.

Here are some things to consider:

Consider any perceived company weaknesses you can turn into strengths. For example, one frustrated business owner frequently got pulled into working in the field alongside his team members because of a lack of help. He recognized he could use this to his advantage when hiring.

When he advertised for help, he positioned this as a strength that would

---

36 - Fleischer, Charles. *HR for Small Business: An Essential Guide for Managers, Human Resources Professionals and Small Business Owners* (2nd Edition), Sphinx Publishing, 2009.

appeal to potential applicants: "We grew up in the business, and we continue to work alongside our employees, so we know what you need to do the job and what you go through daily."

Ask your current A-Player team members what they like most about working for your company. When we bring new clients into our Exclusive Small Group Coaching Program, we survey their best team members and ask these questions. The responses help our clients create Careers pages for their websites and other recruiting materials. Essentially, their A-Players are telling us exactly what they need to say to recruit more A-Players like them.

Once you have this description articulated, you're in a much better position to describe this person. This helps when talking to other team members and when you are networking. It also lets you write job ads that stand out from your competition and attract the right applicants. Here's a great example of a sample Lead Carpenter job posting written by Erin Longmoon of Zephyr Recruiting using Hire the Best™ strategy!

Lead Carpenter Job Description[37]

Are you looking for a truly great place to work? A place where you can use your years of carpentry experience, have fun, and work on beautiful projects? Do you enjoy leading a team to get the job done? Then keep reading, we may be the place for you.

A little about us…we are a well-established, successful, and solid residential Design/Build company in the West Seattle neighborhood. We are a close-knit team, who are authentic, supportive, accountable, friendly, results oriented, talented, and highly skilled.

---

37 - This example is shared graciously by Zephyr Recruiting. Please do not copy it in its entirety for use in your business. Use it as an example to create your customized ad that attracts the ideal team member and culture for which you are recruiting.

Our core values: Integrity, Team Work, and The Golden Rule

Our 4 Pillars of Service: Communication, Experience, Trust, and Integrity – We strive to ALWAYS exceed expectations.

If being a part of this team inspires you, and you share similar values, then please send us your resume, we would love to speak with you.

Here is more about the position:

This is one of the most important roles within our company, the Lead Carpenter is responsible for being the point of contact on a job site for the Project Manager, Carpentry team, Sub-contractors, and clients. This diligent person will keep the team engaged, on-task, on-budget, and most importantly safe; while striving to exceed client expectations.

Essential Functions
- Responsible for the day to day operation on the job site
- Interpret, understand, and follow construction drawings to ensure successful completion of project
- Daily updates to job on Buildertrend application
- Discuss any conflict between plans and site conditions to the Project Manager in a timely manner
- Able to coordinate schedules between subcontractors on a jobsite
- Routinely review production schedule and keep job on-track and on-time
- Ensure job site is always hazard free and clean
- Verify correct selections are being installed or applied
- Coordinate inspections and effectively communicate results

- Following company SOPs with consistent, timely and accurate submission of required paperwork
- Ability to lift up to 60 lbs., work on ladders up to 30 feet off the ground and roofs up to 50 feet off the ground
- Read plans and scope of work to answer questions

Experience and Education
- High School diploma or equivalent
- 7-10 recent years carpentry experience in residential re-modeling and new construction
- Excellent and creative written and oral communication and interpersonal relationship skills
- Proficient use of Tablet functionality and Microsoft and Google applications for job and administrative tasks

Required Skills & Abilities
- Ability to read and interpret schematic designs and construction documents.
- Able to understand unique site characteristics, restrictions and requirements.
- General construction, materials, and tools knowledge.
- Good knowledge of field production rates.
- Ability to prioritize job responsibilities.
- Ability to analyze and effectively solve problems.
- Excellent communication and interpersonal skills.
- Excellent organizational and time management skills.
- Ability to handle adversity and challenges
- Service and teamwork oriented.
- Customer centered and focused.

Behaviors
- Demonstrates integrity
- Strong leadership skills
- Displays initiative
- Takes ownership
- Good listener
- Precise
- Thorough
- Trustworthy
- Resourceful
- Thrives on energy of fast-paced projects
- Collaborative
- Highly competent and confident
- Shows maturity
- Comfortable being transparent
- Humble
- Focused

Thank you for reading through our whole post, it is imperative to us that we find the best match for us, and the best match for you. So, if you still feel you are a great fit for us and this position, then PLEASE submit your resume and a cover letter. In your cover letter please state what most excites you about our company or position.

We have a formal recruiting process and have a relationship with Zephyr Recruiting LLC, whom we use for the screening and hiring process. If you are selected for the next step you will get instructions on what those are within 3 days of your submission. Everyone will be contacted.

We are really excited to get to know you and to see if we are a great match!

Develop Your Culture

Attracting A-Players becomes easier and easier as you intentionally develop a good culture. Every business has a culture. Your Immutable Laws are the building blocks for the culture in your business.

Display your Immutable Laws proudly on your website. Incorporate them in your contracts. It's not enough to list your Immutable Laws and share them prominently. You want to weave these into your everyday conversations with team members, clients, and vendors. How do you do that?

Make use of storytelling to reinforce the culture of your business. Remember the times you felt really proud of something a team member did? There's a great story in there. Tell it . . . over and over. It's okay if your team members think you have dementia because you keep telling the same stories over and over. You are reinforcing your Immutable Laws and creating a culture. Don't worry. Soon you will have more stories to add to your collection. You will be on the lookout for team members' wins and successes with respect to demonstrating your Immutable Laws. When you catch them doing something awesome, or hear that feedback from a client, share the story at your next team meeting. Tie it back to one of your Immutable Laws.

Your core values are also observable outside of your company. For example, I was introduced to Brian Gottlieb by Tony Mancini. When Tony suggested I connect with Brian Gottlieb from Tundraland, he described Brian as a good leader and businessman. But Tony's description of the effect of the culture Brian built at Tundraland made the biggest impression on me. Here is what Tony said:

> *His employees are fanatics. They are absolute fanatics about the company, about what they do, why it's important, the satisfaction they get from it outside of straight compensation. To me, as you look at that next generation of workers, my goodness, there's nothing that's going to be more important than that. It needs to be bigger than the job and compensation, and he's made that. He's created a culture where it's bigger*

than the job and it's bigger than them remodeling. It's much bigger than that. That's almost a byproduct of who they are.

Imagine building a culture so impactful people describe *your* team members that way. Imagine people describing your company that way. Imagine making *that* impression on people.

Diane Hatfield of Hatfield Builders and Remodelers includes respect as an Immutable Law to build a company culture where everyone is treated well. Diane believes in treating her team members with the respect she would like to be treated with. As she puts it:

> *I treat them with the respect that I would want to be treated when I'm working with someone and for someone. I know what it's like to work in a crap environment. Chad does, too. I know what it's like to have a manager that I hated, who micromanaged the crap out of people, who talked down to people, who didn't trust people, and I worked for her for years, and it was awful. We got along because I knew how to manage her managing me. I want to treat our staff members with the love and respect I would want to receive. When we think about things with a cool, level head, and we give them the opportunity to speak and talk and put out their ideas, it becomes more productive, and it becomes a better environment . . . They're not just our staff, our employees, they're really valuable people to us, and we cannot do this without them. This business does not operate the way that we've got it operating right now without them.*

That mindset ensures Chad and Diane create and protect an environment in which high performers can—and will—thrive.

An Inside Look Into What It Really Takes to Create a Great Place to Work

Chuck Parmely of The Overhead Door Co. of Riverton-Lander, in Riverton, Wyoming, has built an amazing place to work. He put his money where his mouth is, too, and submitted his business to be evaluated by *Inc.* magazine to be considered as one of the best places to work. Inc. evaluated Chuck's company and gave them a *glowing* report. But it was not always that glowing.

I have been working with Chuck since 2009. In an interview I conducted with Chuck on the *Profit by Design* podcast, he reflected back on his notes from a January 16, 2009 team meeting. Chuck reflected on telling his team business was slow. His backlog was operating at a fraction of what it used to be. Layoffs were likely. He announced an out-of-town project and asked for volunteers. He informed his crew that those who objected to working out of town would be the most likely to be laid off. Chuck was obviously frustrated. He revealed he had to make cuts because the company was bleeding money. He was cutting company benefits and more.

Chuck was in pain. He was scared. He was panicked. He felt desperate. Looking back, Chuck could not believe the mindset he was in and the impact that created on the environment for his team. He was in such a different place than he is now.

In his interview, Chuck describes how far the company has come since 2009. Everybody's attitude has changed. The team is much more aligned.

Chuck credits the culture they have developed. At the time of *Inc.*'s review of Chuck's business, 92.31% of employees were "highly engaged." Fifteen of sixteen team members were highly engaged. The other team member indicated they were "moderately engaged." Nobody was disengaged.

Their team members sing their praises. One, who had been with the company for less than a year, remarked about how well the team works together to support their clients. He commented about how much support the owner (Chuck) provides their team and how that contributes to each person's success and the company as a whole.

How did Chuck create that culture? Simple. You take care of your employees, and they'll take care of your business. Chuck empowers team members to make decisions.

We do not judge them, even when things go wrong. They turn mistakes into learning experiences and move on. They do not dwell on things. They make sure team members know they care about them and want them to succeed.

If someone makes a poor decision," Chuck said, he does not ask, "Why did you do that?" Instead, he says, "Talk with me about what went into that decision." He explains, "If there is one thing Sabrina has taught me over the years, it is that nobody will think exactly like me. I need to understand them and their way of thinking."

By dropping judgment and taking a more curious and conversational approach, Chuck transformed the energy at his company. Chuck's natural response is to get frustrated that people do not think like him. He has trained himself to flip that mindset to a mindset of curiosity, asking people to talk with him about their decision-making process. That simple mindset shift takes away the judgment and frustration.

Chuck has created a safe, supportive, open culture

105

through simple—but not easy—shifts in his mindset, combined with his willingness to look inward and receive feedback through coaching. He works hard to support their team members, and everyone can see it. Every quarter, they have a meeting called "Wings and Things" where they talk about financial results, have fun, and learn together. These meetings go a long way to make each team member feel important and informed.

Make Your Business an Ideal Place to Work for Your Ideal Team Member

You should know why every A-Player who has worked for you accepted your offer. Why did they choose to work at your business? Find out what they most appreciate about the opportunity to work for you. Ask what benefits they appreciate. You'd be surprised at the little things that matter. I recall a client who took a competitors' A-Player to lunch and asked him what benefits he really appreciated. What was top of his list? Direct deposit of his paycheck. I'm telling you . . . the simplest things make the difference.

When our clients start working with us, we survey their A-Players. I've had the privilege of reading those survey responses for years now. What's at the top of the list of what A-Players appreciate? A boss who cares and listens to them. Regular communication. Simple things. Powerful impact.

Similarly, anytime an A-Player leaves your business, find out why. Don't be afraid to ask this question. You need to know what you can do to improve. A formal exit interview is a good idea. At the very least, ask your team member to share why they are choosing to leave. Sometimes it's as simple as a personal issue you couldn't avoid. Other times, they will share something that helps you avoid similar issues with other A-Players in the future.

Becoming an "Employer of Choice"[38]

A-Players are not just looking for any job. They are looking for a career. These are the four most important qualities A-Players seek from an employer:

- A great boss and coworkers. If you have a large percentage of A-Players working for you, flaunt it! Similarly, if you know why your team members like working for you, share this with prospective team members.
- Interesting, meaningful work
- Growth and opportunity to advance their careers
- Work-life balance

If you offer any or all of these, build this into your recruiting messages. These are the intangible perks of working for you.

A-Players are motivated by the opportunity to move up in your business and advance their careers. **Small businesses are uniquely positioned to offer advancement opportunities to A-Players.**

A-Players like the idea of being able to move into higher-level positions more quickly in small business than in the corporate world and bigger cities.

They like the breadth of the work they get to do in a small business, rather than being confined to a narrow role. They *want* more responsibility and feel good when they can be competent in successfully fulfilling your expectations of them. Often, internal politics and red tape at bigger companies make things takes longer to get things done. Many A-Players can't stand big company politics and prefer to work for a smaller business.

Small businesses also are much better positioned than larger organizations to meet the work-life balance needs of their team members. Why? Small business owners can flexibly address work-life balance with their team members. Larger organizations tend to take a "one size fits all"

---

38 - Be sure to visit *TapThePotential.com/Toolkit* to access the Tap the Potential Great Place to Work Spotlights. These are examples of simple actions small business owners just like you are taking to create a great culture.

approach to this issue, which is very frustrating for team members. According to Stewart Friedman, professor of management and the founding director of the Wharton School's Leadership Program, "It's not an uncommon problem in many HR areas where, for the sake of equality, there's a standard policy that is implemented in a way that is universally applicable—[even though]—everyone's life is different and everyone needs different things in *terms of how to integrate the pieces. It's got to be customized.*[39]"

As a business owner, you have an opportunity to shine as an Employer of Choice in your community. Get to know the unique needs of your team members. Work with them to balance their performance at work with other areas of life that are important to them.

Many successful business owners are doing just that, but not in a formal way. It's just who they are. They care about their team members and work with them when various circumstances arise in the lives of their team members. If this is something you are already doing, it's time to "toot your own horn" and make it more widely known that this is a benefit of working for you.

Making Work Meaningful

How could a bathroom project have deep meaning? Every project does. Every construction project is a place a family will gather, a place children will play, or dinners will be held. But some projects have a much more special meaning. Take this example, shared with me by Brian Gottlieb:

> *You and I take many things for granted on a daily basis, such as taking a shower or taking a bath with safety. Not everyone shares that same experience. Many veterans have mobility issues and are afraid to step into their own bathrooms. It's a dangerous room to them.*

---

39 - Keyser, John. "Are we happy yet: How coaching is improving workplace morale." *Choice* Volume 11, Number 4. pp 19-20, December 2013.

My team and I love to surprise veterans with free bath remodeling projects. We have fun with it and surprise them in cool and different ways. It has become so rewarding our whole company rallies behind these projects and comes together.

Brian and his team at Tundraland also are taking the impact they can have on a community to new heights through their *Windows for a Cause* program.

When they remove windows from homes, local artists turn the windows into pieces of art. They then auction off the art and use the proceeds to make a positive impact on the life of someone in their local community.

In 2017, they used the money to help a local Vietnam War era veteran, John Green. Mr. Green had been stuck in a wheelchair for more than forty years. Tundraland's *Windows for a Cause* initiative raised enough money to buy him a custom wheelchair that allows him to stand up, which he hadn't been able to do for more than four decades.

Tundraland's *Baths for the Brave and Windows for a Cause* programs build a lot of team spirit among their team members. Being involved in projects like these and giving back to veterans puts new meaning to their work. That focus on meaning does not stop with those specific projects, however. It opens people's eyes to look for meaning in other projects, too, especially if you are having conversations with your team about the impact their work has on customers.

Brian and his team do a free project for somebody just about every month. They choose in a fun manner. Any team member can submit a deserving candidate for consideration and then pitch that candidate to be selected. This selection process creates a tremendous amount of pride and ownership among Brian and his team members. Brian describes the impact this has on the culture as "absolutely incredible . . . goosebumps."

Love Wins

Ronda Conger knows how to become an Employer of Choice. As a result of her "love wins" strategy, her company, CBH Homes, won an award as one of Idaho's Best Places to Work in 2017.

If you're a leader of any company, what you believe in and how you operate is going to affect all those around you. I think that's why it's even more important that I firmly believe that love should be at the basis in my opinion . . . if you're in our office, you're going to hear, 'I love you' several times throughout the day through almost every employee. It's our thing. We believe in it. We have these huge inflatable love balls. You're going to laugh, but they're huge. I'm talking like the biggest beach ball you've ever seen, and we have some around the office that say it. Our walls have 'Love wins' on it. We have T-shirts that say, 'Love wins' on them. All the ladies in the office for Christmas got a necklace that says 'Love wins' on it. We've embraced it and put it around us. You see it everywhere.

I feel like that's what has driven me my whole life. I decided a long time ago that love beat every other emotion. It beat fear, or anger, meanness, jealousy, all those other ones. I felt like when you love who you are, you love your company, you love your team, I always say, you love your buyers. You're going to win, right? It's just the highest form, so I think if we keep that first, that's what matters.

I learned this from Darren Hardy, the editor of Success maga-zine. I love what he says: 'We, as humans, are literally walking around with this sign around our neck that says, 'I need love.'' I don't know anyone that's not looking to be treated with kindness, right? To be treated well, to be treated that you're valued, and that you're appreciated.

Ronda shares that their team members are with them, on average, 8.9 years. That's *more than double* the national average of

4.2 years, across all industries, and 4.1 years for construction industry workers according to the U.S. Bureau of Labor Statistics.[40]

Ronda credits team loyalty to the culture they have created. Employees value the culture more than small—and sometimes large—bumps in pay they might get if they went elsewhere. For example, a team member once approached Ronda and said, "I've got this incredible job offer, double the money. I gotta go. I'm so sorry. I love you, I love this place, but man, I've gotta do it." Realizing he was being courted with a number they could not even come close to matching, Ronda replied, "Well, if you have to do it, you have to do it, right? I can't stop you, and I'm not going to pay you double, right? I love you, but good luck."

Eighteen months later, the employee returned to her and said the other job was not what he expected. Money is not the answer. Ronda firmly states, "When people are miserable, the environment's horrible, the culture's horrible, and the leadership's horrible. It doesn't matter how much they pay you." That is exactly what this employee confirmed when he returned, asking for his old job back at his old salary. Ronda brought him back.

Treat people with love and respect. Commit to a shared set of values. This is the glue that will keep your A-Players loyal to your company. Contrary to many people's thinking, employees today stay longer with a company today than they did years ago. For example, in 1998, average tenure was 3.6 years, according to the U.S. Bureau of Labor Statistics, more than half a year less than it was in 2018.[41]

The construction industry has seen an even greater increase in tenure.

---

40 - *https://www.bls.gov/news.release/tenure.t05.htm*

41 - *https://www.bls.gov/news.release/history/tenure_092498.txt*

In 2008, the average construction worker was with their current employer for 3.5 years. In 2018, the average increased to 4.1 years.[42]

These rises can be traced back further, too. The truth is, while it might feel as if people are staying with their companies for shorter periods of time, the numbers prove otherwise. Even through deep recessions, people want to stay with their companies. If you become an Employer of Choice, like Ronda has developed, you too can reap the benefits of low turnover and increased loyalty.

> **Treat people with love and respect. Commit to a shared set of values. This is the glue that will keep your A-Players loyal to your company.**

The Value of 1:1 Meetings

Make time for conversations with your team members to find out what matters to them. It really is that simple. Weekly 1:1 meetings with your team go a long way toward creating a culture where team members feel connected, appreciated, and supported.

At a minimum, every team member should meet with a supervisor once per week for a short focused one-on-one discussion. Team meetings should happen weekly. Make use of technology, such as Zoom, to bridge distances between office locations and make it easy for those in the field to participate. For my guide to *Short and Sweet Weekly Meetings*, including meeting agenda templates, visit the Toolkit at *www.TapThePotential.com/Toolkit*.

Although it may sound daunting to carve out the time to make these

---

42 - *https://www.bls.gov/news.release/tenure.t05.htm*

happen, ultimately, it's going to free up more of your time as your team becomes more capable and confident. Your trust level will go up as well. Regular meetings make it easy to address the small matters that can quickly turn into big issues and lead to an A-Player quitting or getting fired. As Mike Bruno shares,

> *Never lose sight of open and honest communication. Communication is very, very important both ways. Do not let things build up inside of you when something is wrong. You will destroy your company and your personal life. Bringing negative things home and complaining to your wife or a friend does nothing. You need to address whatever's happening in your company right away with productive communication—with a conversation, not yelling, not berating, not focused around negativity, but open and honest communication.*

Ronda Conger meets with over eighty team members at least once per year. "I want to know how their whole life is. I know everyone's kids. I know everyone's spouses. I know a little bit about their background, what they come from, what they believe in, what they're struggling with." Ronda recently implemented voluntary monthly Leadership Coffees, starting at 6:30 a.m. At least fifty team members showed up at the last one.

Onboarding A-Players for Loyalty and Engagement

Onboarding new team members is your greatest opportunity to lay the foundation for trust and loyalty with your new team member. Yet in the rush to fill open roles to meet client and project obligations, the process typically happens informally, in a haphazard way. Many owners undermine engagement and loyalty during a team member's critical first ninety days by being careless.

Before you start the hiring process, think through your own needs from a new team member and their needs and expectations as a member of your team.

Intentionally design your onboarding system. Determine what success will look like one year from now. Imagine you have an A-Player in the role you are filling. What results is that person achieving at the end of year one?

Now reverse-engineer your expectations. What results are they achieving at nine months into their new job? Six months? Ninety days? Month one? Week one? And day one? Lay out your expectations of them. Share this during the interview. You are showing them clear performance criteria. You can tie the criteria to clear opportunities for advancement with your company.

Use the performance criteria through year one as your initial outline of a training plan to bring your new team member up to speed as quickly as possible. Recall the Engagement Matrix I shared earlier in the book. The goal of onboarding is to move your team member from the EI Quadrant to the EE Quadrant as quickly as possible, then keep them there. Most business owners are very inefficient in bringing new team members up to speed. So, profitability suffers long term. A clear training plan allows you to ramp up team members much faster, which has a significant impact on their productivity. Have loyal team members, reduced turnover, and growing profit. Designing your onboarding system now lays the foundation for years to come.

Get into the right frame of mind when looking to bring on new employees. Take things slow and invest in building a culture full of training and support with each new hire. As Mike puts it:

> *When you hire somebody new, it's so much more than just filling a position. Let's take hiring a carpenter as an example. If I hire a carpenter tomorrow, he's going to have a resume, and he's going to tell me that he's the greatest carpenter and wants to make $35.00 an hour. I can send him somewhere, but how do I know if his production standards are going to be in place? How do I know if the rate of production is going to be in line with what I need?*
>
> *There needs to be a ramp-up process. There need to be culture*

discussions. There needs to be a conversation in which you tell candidates, 'This is what our small business is about. This is how I want you to communicate. This is what our requirement is,' before you bring people on. Follow that with a very strict review process, at thirty, sixty, ninety, and 120 days after hiring. Be open and honest during those evaluations. Let them know what you are seeing and where that new employee stands with key metrics. There needs to be metrics in place to be able to identify those A-Players.

Tell each new team member what to expect. Say, 'You're being hired for this reason, to support the company in this fashion. When we have our weekly meeting or our monthly meeting, we're going to talk about these things to make sure that you're on track, and you're developing in a productive manner and also producing what needs to be produced for the company.' This will remove the potential for a surprise when constructive feedback inevitably arises.

By laying this groundwork with each candidate, you set the right expectations from the start. Maintaining regular 1:1 and weekly team meetings makes it natural for constructive feedback to be received and applied. That gives you the opportunity to turn good team members into great ones instead of making them feel as if they are failing and need to look for another job.

Remember, when you take exceptional care of your team, they will take exceptional care of your clients and customers.[43]

> "The new breed of loyalty will be based upon an understanding between employees and companies of one another's purpose— to become the best version of themselves."
> —Matthew Kelly, The Dream Manager

---

43 - For support in designing your onboarding system and first year experience for new hires, we offer a course, A-Player Onboarding: The Proven System for Driving Loyalty, Engagement and Success, at Tap the Potential. Visit *www.TapThePotential.com/Onboarding.*

Develop Your Team

Many business owners miss a subtle yet critical shift in their role once they move from being the only one in the business to bringing on team members. Once you have team members on board, your greatest responsibility is to develop your team. It is no longer about you doing the work. It is now about you supporting your team in doing the work.

What support does your team need from you to deliver exceptional results to your clients and customers?

Team development must be an ongoing initiative if you are going to create a great place to work. Team development is your biggest, most effective tool to combat losing A-Players to your competitor down the street who offers to pay more.

Let me ask you . . . what are the hopes and dreams of your team members? You need to know this. If you want your team members to buy into your vision and be part of bringing your vision to fruition, you have to buy in to their hopes and dreams. Beyond buying in to their hopes and dreams, you need to be supporting them in achieving their hopes and dreams. Think about this as a team member . . . **wouldn't you feel loyalty toward a leader who invests time and money to helping you achieve your highest potential?**

This creates a mutually beneficial relationship. That is not the typical transactional, tit-for-tat relationship most employers have with employees. In a transactional relationship, you work, I pay you. There is no loyalty there. You get offered $1 more per hour by my competitor, and of course you're going to take it.

In contrast, in a mutually beneficial relationship, we are invested in one another's success.

In fact, money is not as much of a motivator as we might believe. In 2018, Purdue University wanted to determine the relationship between happiness and income. Researchers took data from the Gallup World Poll, a representative sample of over 1.7 million people worldwide.[44] The study found

---

44 - *https://www.nature.com/articles/s41562-017-0277-0*

optimal emotional well-being occurred when people earned between $60,000 and $75,000 per year. *Declines* in emotional well-being and life satisfaction occurred as people crossed $95,000 per year. Once basic needs are taken care of, money is not a significant motivator.

Psychologist Abraham Maslow identified a basic hierarchy, or pyramid, of human needs. At the base of the pyramid are our basic needs for food, water, and shelter. Once our basic needs are met, we are able to advance up the hierarchy to focus on meeting higher level needs, such as safety. Beyond safety, we become concerned with belongingness and then esteem.

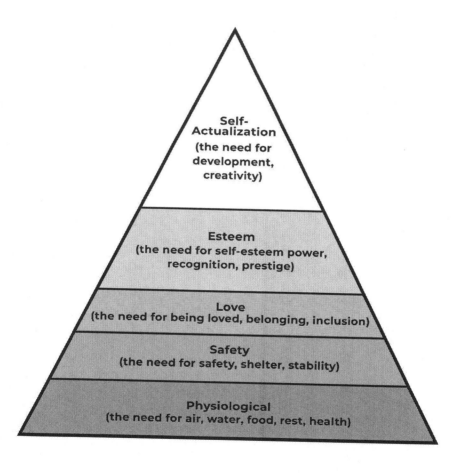

Feelings of emotional safety and belongingness are significant motivators if one has basic needs met. In other words, if your team members are earning a living wage, a bump in pay is not going to motivate an A-Player to take a job elsewhere. This flies in the face of the word on the street. It says entire crews change shirts, abandoning one company to go work for another for a few dollars more per hour.

Here's something to be curious about: Were those A-Players who "changed shirts" in a good company culture? Did they go because they would earn more? Or because they earned more, had real opportunities for advancement, *and* went to work for a company with a better culture?

Your A-Players like to be compensated fairly for the value they bring to your company. They want real opportunities for advancement (not just empty promises). And they love a great company culture where they feel appreciated and a sense of belonging while contributing to the team effort. If you provide those things, you are golden. It's really that simple. Yet, while it's simple, it is not easy for the typical business owner to pull off.

Increasing Loyalty to Drive Productivity and Profit

In their book, *Why Loyalty Matters: The Groundbreaking Approach to Rediscovering Happiness, Meaning and Lasting Fulfillment in Your Life and Work,* Timothy Keiningham and Lerzan Aksoy contend, "The long-term success of any company depends heavily upon the quality and loyalty of its people."[45] Among other points, Keiningham and Askoy shared insights from two well-known studies into the impact of employee loyalty on company performance.

---

45 - Keiningham, Timothy L., and Lerzan Aksoy. *Why Loyalty Matters: The Groundbreaking Approach to Rediscovering Happiness, Meaning and Lasting Fulfillment in Your Life and Work.* Dallas, TX: Benbella Books, 2010.

First, they shared insights from Harvard Business School professors Leonard A. Schlesinger, James L. Heskett, W. Earl Sasser, and Benjamin Schneider. In the 1990s, they began talking about the impact of employee loyalty on performance.[46] In no uncertain terms, they contended, "Employee loyalty drives productivity." They identify employee loyalty one of four critical elements of performance in satisfying customer needs. As Keiningham and Askoy put it, **"Loyal employees are more willing to suppress short-term demands for the long-term benefit of the organization."**

What does this mean? Your team member is more likely to work late on Friday afternoon if she believes in your team's mission of creating a positive impact for your customer. It means your sales associate will forgo making the sale and a commission if the sale is not in the best interests of your customer. The team member will not jeopardize a long-term relationship. It means your team members look out for the needs of your customers and identify ways to serve them better.

The cumulative impact of these actions cannot be underestimated. It's no wonder that a Harvard study of 200 companies identified that a strong culture increases net income more than 750% over ten years.[47]

Keiningham and Askoy also discuss a study by Professor Benjamin Schneider of the University of Maryland. The study was on the impact of employee loyalty and attitude on performance. It was called *Which Comes First: Employee Attitudes or Organizational Financial and Market Performance?*[48] Professor Schneider and his team studied thirty-five companies over eight years. They found positive loyalty-related attitudes in employees led to better company performance.

46 - Heskett, J., W.E. Sasser Jr., and L. Schlesinger. *The Service Profit Chain: How Leading Companies Link Profit and Growth to Loyalty, Satisfaction, and Value.* New York: Free Press, 1997.

47 - Coyle, Daniel. "Introduction: When Two Plus Two Equals Ten." *The Culture Code: the Secrets of Highly Successful Groups*, Bantam, 2018, p. xviii. See also Kotter, J. P., and J.L. Heskett. Corporate Culture and Performance. New York: Free Press, 1992.

48 - Schneider, Benjamin, Paul J. Hanges, D. Brent Smith, and Amy Nicole Salvaggio. "Which Comes First: Employee Attitudes or Organizational Financial and Market Performance?" *Journal of Applied Psychology* 88, no. 5 (2003): 836–51. *https://doi.org/10.1037/0021-9010.88.5.836.*

Reducing turnover costs and increasing productivity increase your profitability. I cannot overstate the benefit of investing in finding *and retaining* the best talent possible for your company through developing a strong culture. When you do, your team will become more loyal and your performance will improve. Also, the culture you create by doing so will serve you well when you look for more A-Players to join your team. **This is what it means to create a highly profitable, great place to work!**

Let's face it, you as the owner are juggling a number of demands that threaten to pull your attention down Maslow's hierarchy. Late-night worries about cash flow, meeting payroll, and struggles with subs and vendors keep you operating at the bottom of the hierarchy. Your team needs you to be focusing further up the hierarchy on creating feelings of safety (physical and emotional) and belonging. This principle guides our work with clients in Tap the Potential's Exclusive Small Group Coaching Program. We help our clients focus their efforts in the business. First, we ensure there is a system in place to assure good cash flow. Then we help our clients create the systems and structure to assure smooth operations. They can then put their attention to leadership and team development.

Additionally, we offer several programs to support you in developing your team. One of our most popular programs, Leadership Bootcamp, came about because a client shared with me that although he was learning and growing as a leader through the coaching he was doing, he was having a hard time getting his team on board with the improvements he was trying to make in his company. He asked for a "translator" who could talk with his team and help them "get it." In Leadership Bootcamp, team members with leadership potential come to appreciate their role in creating a highly profitable, great place to work. We teach them about what is really needed from them and how to be more effective as team members.

Business owners rave about the transformation they see in team members in just the course of six clinics. Really, what's happening is the business owner no longer feel like the "lone nut" in the company trying to make things better. Now there are two, then three . . . because the emerging leaders are showing other team members how to be effective at work and be part of the greater vision of the leader.[49]

Through the Tap the Potential Leadership Bootcamp and our Exclusive Small Group Coaching Program, we are supporting our clients in improving communication with their teams, helping their team members work from strengths (that's where tremendous opportunity lies to increase efficiency and productivity in your team), and create coaching cultures. You can learn more about these programs at *www.TapThePotential.com*.

For ideas to develop your team and build culture, check out Tap the Potential's Great Place to Work Spotlights in the accompanying Toolkit (*www.TapThePotential.com/Toolkit*). In these spotlights, I feature business owners doing simple things that are enhancing their company culture. I hope they give you some ideas of what you can be doing.

Best Practices for Retaining A-Players

- Compensate fairly for the value they bring to your company.
- Provide real opportunities for advancement (not just empty promises).
- Create a great company culture where team members feel appreciated and experience a sense of belonging.

---

49 - If you have never seen the video, *Leadership Lessons from Dancing Guy*, by entrepreneur and founder of CD Baby, Derek Sivers, visit *https://youtu.be/fW8amMCVAJQ* or *https://sivers.org/ff* today. Sivers shares a three-minute video beginning with one person dancing alone in a field. Over the course of the three-minute video, the "lone nut" attracts a first follower, then a second, and third. Before you know it, the entire crowd is dancing together. The video is a great example of how we can create positive momentum and impact in our businesses by transforming one team member, then two, then three. But we must make the first move by being the "lone nut" in our businesses. The lone nut then has the responsibility of showing the first follower how to lead.

Best Practices for Getting the Results You Want While Building a Thriving Culture

- Set expectations for the role and put key performance indicators in place—before hiring.
- Communicate your expectations and your Immutable Laws during the interview.
- Clarify training and performance expectations for day one, week one, thirty days, ninety days, 180 days, nine months, and twelve months.
- Quickly address performance gaps. Do not keep new team members who are failing to hit performance targets.
- Each team member should meet weekly with a supervisor for a 1:1.
- Meet weekly as a team.

Brian Gottlieb on Developing Your Team

It starts by really analyzing a sustainable strategy. What is a sustainable strategy in business? It's so easy to look to your product as part of your strategy when in fact products come and go. How do you make strategy an operational point of differentiation?

So, when we look at an operational point of differentiation, that means the people inside of an organization. And therefore, how do we create more than just a job for people? How do we create a career path? How do I get my employees to treat your home as if it's their own? And that's just a fundamentally different way of looking at the business.

In my view, if somebody's in the kitchen business or in

> the bath business, they make money off of selling kitchens or selling baths. And I think there's a decision that has to be made: Are you trying to make money off of a transactional sale, or are you trying to make money by building a lifelong customer?

Make It Easy for the Right Candidates to Get in While Keeping the Wrong Candidates Out

You are the gatekeeper for a great culture. Remember this. It's very important. Do not let the riff-raff in.

Anything worth having is worth working for, right? In a tight labor market, it's easy to fall into the trap of marketing heavily to recruit team members and come across as desperate. You and I know you're working your tail off, and you are desperate for some help so you can take a vacation. Let's just keep that between us for now, okay? From here out, all recruiting messaging is about the *opportunity* to work for you, an Employer of Choice.

Think about how the Marines recruit. They don't advertise that they pay for college or that they teach a valuable skill. Every ad has one simple message: the Marines offer you the opportunity to be challenged physically, mentally, and morally. We target men and women of character. Their motto: Semper Fidelis, means "always faithful" or "always loyal." The Marines are known for their loyalty. We can learn from that.

You want to set up your screening process to be friendly to those who are referred to you while quickly screening out those who are a poor fit. For a deeper dive into how to do this, listen to my interview with Mike Ciavolino of Shore Creative Group. Mike specializes in recruitment marketing. You can listen to his interview on the Profit by Design podcast available from our Toolkit at *www.TapThePotential.com/Toolkit*.

Ronda Conger calls their interview process "The Gauntlet." She identifies the interview process as key to getting good people on her team:

> *I usually have three to four other people interview the candidate. We do a phone interview, we do a video interview, we do a field interview, and we normally do two office interviews. We call our process 'the gauntlet' and we mean that. We're looking for certain traits. I have the 12 traits of a CBH team member.*

Ronda and her team write these traits down and keep them front and center during the interview. They ask themselves, "Does this person possess these traits?"

Your application and interview processes are key to ensuring you are letting in the team members who are a good fit, while screening out those who will undermine the culture you are creating. Learning to interview effectively is a skillset, just like any other skillset we acquire in business. It does take practice, and it helps tremendously to know what to ask, why you are asking it, and the subtleties of what to pay attention to in the responses of the candidates and references.

The book, *Who*, by Geoff Smart, goes in depth about the interview process, along with the questions to ask. We follow this process in my company, and many of our clients do as well. In addition, I teach interview skills and best practices in my online course that accompanies this book. As a psychologist and observer of human behavior, I've honed in on the simple interview techniques that help small business owners find out if the candidate really is that A-Player who will be a good fit. You can access my course at *www.TapThePotential.com/Course.*

Inoculate Your Candidates

No matter how great your culture is, there are difficult aspects of working in your company and challenging aspects of each role. Earlier we talked about the downside of "selling" your company to candidates. Avoid selling candidates on your company. Be brutally honest with candidates about what it is like to work for you—from the very start.

Tell applicants ahead of time and let them screen themselves out before they even fill out an application. This will save you a lot of time, frustration, and heartache. When applicants know the challenges ahead of time and accept them, they are much more likely to persevere when they encounter them. This reduces turnover.

What are the most difficult and frustrating aspects of the job a successful candidate will be asked to do?

So, what is it about working for you and doing what you will ask your team member to do that is hard, difficult, or challenging? Ask your best team members. Let them know you want to attract more team members, who like them, are more than willing to work through the hardest parts of the job. If you're a roofing company in the deep south, your candidates need to know what it *really* feels like to be on a roof in August and why you start at daybreak.

Complete the description for your ideal candidate for a position. Then use your requirements to help people disqualify themselves or commit to your standards.

Getting a flu shot bolsters your body's ability to fight the flu. Inoculate your applicants by letting them know about the hardest parts of the job. This greatly increases the likelihood they will deal with challenges with minimal complaint. Your best team members will be proud of the challenges they overcome in working for you!

Make Employment Offers That Can't Be Matched

Because A-Players will be in demand and likely still employed, you can do everything right only to lose the candidate to a better offer from their current employer or an offer from a different employer. This happens frequently. Expect it when you make your offer.

You can reduce the risk of this happening by making offers that *can't* be matched. Make a better financial offer to the candidate. In addition, you also should offer things you know someone's employer can't match. It requires a bit more digging during the interview process to identify these things. When you find yourself across the table from someone you believe to be a true A-Player, ask what would put them in a better position to succeed.

For example, many employers ask candidates why they're considering leaving their current employer. That's a good question to ask for many reasons. If a candidate says they're looking because there are no opportunities to grow, you need to demonstrate tangible opportunities to grow.

Listen carefully to candidates about why they're considering leaving their current employer. Get them talking about things money can't buy. These include vacation time, the ability to work from home some days, or other fringe benefits you can offer that their employer can't or doesn't offer.

Then frame the conversation around the things you can offer that their current employer cannot match simply by bumping their pay. Prepare your candidate: their employer may increase their pay or offer a promotion once the candidate gives notice. Ask how the candidate will handle that. As the candidate describes their plan to leave because you are a better opportunity, they solidify their commitment.

Now that you have greater clarity on who is an A-Player for your business and ways to attract A-Players to your team, it's time to find these people. Yes, they exist, and you may be closer to hiring them than you realize!

What's Possible . . .

What's possible when you're attracting a steady stream of A-Players because you are an Employer of Choice?

Just imagine . . .

What's possible for you?

What's possible for your business?

Chapter 4
Where to Find Your A-Players

"A-Players are rarely unemployed. You have to get strategic to attract them to work for you."
—Dr. Sabrina Starling

I really want to hire the best, but where do I find them?

Tapping into the networks of A-Players on your team is the most effective way to attract the best team members to your business. Here's why: your best team members likely hold values very similar to your Immutable Laws. That's why you work well together. That is the effect of shared values.

And here's some good news: A-Players tend to associate with one another. When you find one A-Player, you can tap into that person's network and get to know even more A-Players. A-Players hang together!

It's our human nature to gravitate toward other like-minded individuals.

There's another benefit of networking through your A-Players to attract more team members: reduced turnover. There's a dramatic difference between team members who are referred to your business and those who are hired through job boards and career sites. Specifically, after one year, 46% of employees hired through referrals remain in their jobs.[50] Compare that to just 33% from career sites and 22% from job boards.

After two years, 45% of employees hired through referrals remain in their jobs. Only 20% of employees hired from career sites and job boards

---

50 – *https://www.ere.net/10-compelling-numbers-that-reveal-the-power-of-employee-referrals/*

are still in their jobs. After three years, that number shrunk to just 14%.

Although it may take a bit of effort to kick off your intentional networking to attract A-Players, over time, recruiting becomes much easier. If you do this type of networking at the same time you are intentionally creating a great place to work, you will discover that hiring exceptional team members gets easier. Word spreads. We'll talk about creating a great place to work later in the book, but first let's turn our attention to tapping into the A-Player network to recruit.

I have more good news for you . . . you are not limited to the A-Players on your team. You are connected to multiple A-Players' networks. You can tap into each of these to bring you your next great team member.

The A-Player Networks

In his book, *Friend of a Friend*, David Burkus explains how important personal networks have been for some of the most successful people in the world. Successful people know they need to surround themselves with other people who can help them develop and grow. Quality personal networks can work the same for you, especially when it comes to hiring.

Remember this: A-Players hang together.

You are an A-Player. I know this because you picked up this book, and you've read to this point. Do you know most business owners don't read? Of those who do read, many never get past the first chapter or two. So, I can say with confidence, you've made it here. You're an A-Player. This means you have networks of A-Players around you. Each member in your A-Player network knows more A-Players. Those A-Players likely belong to networks of other A-Players.

You've heard the saying, "It's a small world," and that really is true when it comes to networking. But what you may not realize is just how small our world really is when social media is used to enhance our networking.

Burkus reveals how closely connected each of us actually is. If you have a

Facebook account, you likely are fewer than four introductions away from anyone else within Facebook's billion-plus network.[51] Let that sink in for a moment. You could be just a handful of introductions away from your next hire.

We need to think beyond our immediate networks. This is where most of us stop short and overlook significant opportunity to find the A-Players we are seeking. According to Burkus, our weaker ties, those with whom we rarely connect for years or decades, may be our most valuable connections. The reason is that the people we know best typically know the same people we know. "Our weak ties often build a bridge from one cluster to another and thus give us access to new information." He continues, "Even though the strong ties in our life are more likely to be motivated to help us, it turns out that our weak ties' access to new sources of information might be more valuable."

Who do you know in your network whom you haven't spoken to in a few years? Pick up the phone and give them a call. Invite them to lunch or coffee. Most likely in the course of catching up, you will be asked what you are up to these days. That's the perfect opportunity. Share that your company is growing, and you are looking to be introduced to _____ (fill in the blank with your description of an A-Player for the roles you anticipate filling).

Beyond your weak ties, recognize that your current A-Player team members have the potential to serve as "brokers." Burkus says brokers are people who span gaps between groups and create connections with people outside their immediate cluster. **Brokers likely exist within your current team, your top customers, your colleagues and friends, and even your vendor network.**

---

51 - Specifically, as Burkus discusses on page 45 of *Friend of a Friend*, Facebook began a study in 2011 to track the degrees of separation between users. Facebook posted 721 million users at the time and found the degree of separation between users to be 3.74 people. In other words, on average, Facebook could connect any user on Facebook to any other user on Facebook in fewer than four connections. To borrow from Burkus' book title, in 2011 the average Facebook user was a "friend of a friend of a friend of a friend" of every other Facebook user. When Facebook ran the study again in 2016, the number of users had more than doubled to 1.59 billion and the degree of separation between two users decreased to 3.57 people. The "friend of a friend" principle is a powerful one. (Burkus, David. *Friend of a Friend . . .: Understanding the Hidden Networks That Can Transform Your Life and Your Career.* Boston: Houghton Mifflin Harcourt, 2018, page 45.)

Your best team members hold the initial clues to finding more A-Players.[52] Get to know your best team members better. The added benefit is that your team members will be honored that you care enough to want to get to know them better and want their input. Discover and tap into their networks. These networks are jumping off points to help you find more great team members.

Here are some questions to get you started in getting to know your best team members better:

- When you first applied, how did you hear about us and the open position? (These answers provide clues to referral sources and places to advertise for future applicants).
- Why did you come to work for us? (These answers are clues to what make it attractive for an A-Player to work for you versus another employer).
- What do you like most about your job and about our company? (More clues for what makes your business attractive to A-Players).
- What clubs and community organizations do you belong to? (Pay attention—this is where to start networking and recruiting. Hint: Get your team members involved in community organizations, and let them recruit for you!)
- What social media sites do you use? (Discover where A-Players are connecting. Show up there. Share helpful tips, resources, and educational content pertaining to the interests of your A-Players. Tag your A-Players in company posts. This increases the likelihood of showing up in their networks.)
- Who are the A-Players you know? (Keep in mind, these people are likely employed and are not seeking work right now. However, they may be seeking better opportunities. Connect with them. Build a relationship. Add value in their world so they come to see you as an Employer of Choice within their circle.)

---

52 - Smart, Bradford D. *Topgrading: The Proven Hiring and Promoting Method That Turbocharges Company Performance* (3rd Edition). New York: Portfolio/Penguin, 2012.

As a general rule of thumb, **A-Players "hang" together** in their social circles. With a bit of innovation and organization, you'll become more effective in recruiting the best team members.

What if you're the only A-Player in your company?

If you are the only A-Player you can identify in your business, start there. Tap into your networks. You know other A-Players. They know other A-Players, too.

Think about the groups to which you belong: professional organizations, the Chamber of Commerce, Kiwanis, Rotary, your church, neighborhood association, or kids' baseball team. These are just some of the many networks of which you are a part.

Another option for finding help is *NextDoor.com*, which connects people living or working in local communities with each other. Neighbors use it to recommend contractors, share resources, or organize community activities. You could use it to find talented A-Players who might be looking for new opportunities.

You're probably thinking, *"But, Sabrina, they have jobs. They aren't interested in working for me."* Maybe . . . or maybe not. You'll never know if you *assume* they can't help you fill your openings. Even if they aren't interested, chances are, they may know someone who would be interested.

If you have done your homework to describe your ideal team member, you can easily describe the type of person you are seeking. You can ask if they know of anyone like that. Even if the person they know is currently employed, you can ask that they put you in touch with that person so you can introduce yourself. That person may seek you out in the future. What's more, that person may know another A-Player who is looking for exactly what you offer.

This is the **chaining effect** that happens with effective networking.

You want to take advantage of "chaining" when you are networking to connect with A-Players.

> **Never consider one contact a dead-end.** Get in the habit of asking, "Who do you know who might be interested in an opportunity like the one we are offering?"

Discover Your Pool of Ideal Team Members

Did you know the opportunity to work for you is the answer to somebody's prayers?

It may surprise you to learn there is a pool of *your* ideal team members just waiting for the opportunity to work for you. They just don't know about you yet.

Just who are these people, and where do they hang out? That is what you need to figure out.

Who needs the opportunity you are offering? Even more importantly, what *groups* of people need the opportunity you are offering? Beyond that, where do these people gather? In other words, *what are the "congregation points" for these individuals who are potentially ideal team members for you?*

This is easier once you have thought through the qualities you are looking for in a team member and what makes you unique as an employer.

Let me share an example to illustrate this concept. One business owner in the industry found himself in a real pinch a couple of years ago. He needed team members to fulfill his contracts, but the applicants just weren't showing up. He was facing a lot of competition from the oilfield and it was not at all unusual for a new hire to show up for work for a week or two then just disappear after taking a higher-paying job in the oilfield. In a pinch, this owner hired a couple of his wife's friends to fill positions in his crews.

As I worked with him, he came to see that a solution he perceived as a simple effort to solve a problem in a pinch might actually be developed into a long-term solution that would allow him to expand his business.

The female team members stayed with his company longer, were more reliable on a day-to-day basis, and were more conscientious in maintaining his equipment. When he placed them on crews with male team members, those crews worked more efficiently than the all-male crews. Although there were some duties the female team members could not carry out due to the physical requirements, when they were placed on crews with male team members, their male counterparts were able to complete those tasks.

Through our work together, my client decided he would speak with these female team members and find out what they liked about working for him. They were earning higher wages than they had in previous retail and restaurant positions. He already knew this, but something else he discovered through these conversations really surprised him. The seasonal nature of the work was an "intangible perk" for these women.

Up to this point, my client had perceived the seasonal nature of his business as a liability as he could not offer his team members year-round full-time employment. These women told him they actually appreciated the seasonal nature of the work. It allowed them to work hard a few months out of the year to add to the family income and still be available for after-school activities and other family obligations during much of the year. For these women, the opportunity my client provided was an answer to their prayers.

My client decided he could fill a couple more open positions with female team members. He asked his team members if they had friends who might be a good fit for the company. Sure enough, one of the women had two friends who had been stay-at-home moms, but now that their children were in school, they were looking to get back to work. Neither of these women wanted to work full-time, and both were very excited to learn of the opportunity to earn a high wage working full-time 4–5 months out of the year. After they were hired, both confided in my client that working for him really was an ideal solution to bringing more income into their household while still being available for family commitments much of the year. One even commented, "It's the perfect balance!"

With each hire, my client is becoming more well-known as an Employer of Choice among this network of mothers of school-aged children. He used this network to not only hire more female team members, but also to fill other positions on his crew. Just recently he immediately filled an open position by hiring the husband of one of his female employees' friends.

By getting creative, my client was able to tap into an extensive network to fill his open positions. He identified one commonality—that they all have school-age children and want to contribute to their household income in a significant way but do not want to work full-time, year round.

These mothers were not searching for work on Indeed or ZipRecruiter. They were not reading ads on Craigslist. Their "congregation points" are more informal. His female team members are connected through sports events, after-school activities, and social media. My client does not participate in these school activities or sports events, and he does not use social media, so he never encountered these women. Instead, he asked his best team members if they had friends who would be a good fit with the company. His best team members served as brokers introducing him to their network of social contacts.

The more curious my client became to understand the particular needs of his best team members, the more he became aware that he provides an ideal solution to their desire to contribute to the family income without working full-time, year-round. When he featured this opportunity on the Careers page of his website, applications started coming in regularly.

We surveyed his team members again and learned something that surprised us . . . both the male and female team members repeatedly commented on how they appreciate this is a "real family friendly" atmosphere. One team member commented, "We don't curse around here. We treat each other with respect. No one yells at me. It's a family atmosphere. A lot of places give lip service to that, but this is the real deal."

He now has more qualified applicants wanting to work for him than he has open positions. He never advertises. It's all happening through word of mouth.

Every business has a different culture and offers different opportunities for its team members. Discovering your pool of ideal team members starts by getting to know your best team members and why they like working for you. I have compiled several tools you need to jumpstart this effort in the Hire the Best Toolkit™ (*www.TapThePotential.com/Toolkit*).

Attracting and Keeping the Best Team Members for Your Entry-Level Positions

Many small business owners find it difficult to fill entry-level positions. There is much competition for unskilled labor. That can leave you feeling pressured to compete with wages paid by larger employers. When you are maxing out on what you can afford to pay an entry-level employee and still be profitable, it's time to consider other perks.

Small businesses have a *key* advantage over corporate employers, but very few owners recognize it much less leverage it. A great employee can advance their career more rapidly in a small business than in a larger corporation. As Tony Mancini points out, "Everyone I know in this industry loves this industry and tends to stay there for a really long time." There is a lot of opportunity to turn a job in construction into a career of choice.

Many businesses advertise the "opportunity for advancement." Yet, very few small business owners give much thought to what this really means. Fewer have a clear path from an entry-level position through the ranks of the company.

Keep in mind, the best team members are interested in advancing their career. You are at risk of losing your best team members when they don't know how they can advance with your business.

The next time you are hiring an entry-level employee, here are some questions to consider:

- What is the next promotion for this employee?

- What is the pay increase for that promotion?
- What criteria must that employee meet to receive a promotion?
- What personality strengths are needed to perform exceptionally well in the next position?
- What skills are needed?
- Will you provide the training needed to acquire those skills? If not, how will you support that employee in acquiring the necessary training?

Keep asking yourself this same set of questions for each promotion as an entry-level employee advances in your company. You will be in the position to tell an applicant about *real c*areer opportunities with you.

Consider the difference between telling an applicant, "We start you at $15/hour, and you have the opportunity to advance with us" versus "We start you at $15/hour, and if you work hard, over the course of the next 5–7 years, we'll support you in moving up into a management-level position, with the opportunity to earn $90,000 or more annually." The second scenario will be much more attractive to a career-minded applicant, making it more likely you will attract and retain an A-Player employee for your entry-level position.

> **TIP:** Make the first promotion easily achievable for a team member who is a real go-getter. This is psychologically motivating and will increase your odds of retaining that employee over time.

Employee Referral Incentive Programs

If a team member is talking to others about how great it is to work for you, reward that, even if they have yet to hand over an applicant. Reward the behavior you want more of. Incentivize them for making referrals. Train them to look at their networks and those of their family and friends.

If your best team members are trained to spot top talent and refer them to you, it can be one of your most effective ways of attracting great people. They can become your brokers to other networks.

Train, encourage, and reward your A-Players to act as brokers. There's a good chance they will start to see A-Player networks outside of their immediate network and begin to make even more connections to top talent. Over time, this can lead to you having plenty of exceptional team members ready for hire as your needs grow.

In some ways, your A-Players can operate like headhunters, only they often do a better job of finding true A-Players who are a good fit for your company. Your A-Players know your needs and culture. Plus, they have vested interest in bringing you the best. After all, they don't want to work with warm bodies.

Establishing a referral incentive program helps you take advantage of the circles your best team members run in. Burkus might describe them as friends of friends of friends. Your referral incentive program gets your current team members motivated to recruit for you by offering them a reward.

Growing through employee referrals also helps reduce turnover, which will be a major benefit to you in the future. Team members who come from referrals stay longer. They already know someone on the job. They know what they are getting into because their friend described everything to them beforehand.

Educate your team members about who is an ideal team member for the positions you want to fill.

Ask A-Player team members who else they know who they would consider to be an A-Player (at former jobs, from clubs and organizations they are in, etc.).

Here are a couple of pointers about employee referral incentive systems:
- Customize the incentives you give. One employee may value a day off to spend with their kids in the summer. Another may like a gym membership. These incentives don't have to cost you much; just zero in on what your team members like.

- Give the incentive upon the actual hire of the new employee.
- To increase your chance of keeping A-Players, give the referring employee an incentive on anniversary dates of the other employee.

Let's look at an example of how an employee referral incentive program might work. Your employee, Joe, recommended Tim to work for you. Tim turns out to be a real A-Player. You hire Tim and give Joe a gift certificate to take his wife to dinner at a fancy restaurant on Valentine's Day. You did this because Joe is a newlywed. Joe is thrilled! You've made him look really good in his new wife's eyes.

Six months pass, and Tim is rocking and rolling. He's fully trained and doing the work of four team members you let go because they had been doing just enough to get by. You drop a note in Joe's box telling him how thrilled you are with Tim, thanking him again for bringing Tim to the company.

Joe reads the note and checks in with Tim. Joe is now very invested in making sure his buddy Tim is happy with working for you. Plus, Joe likes working with Tim. Joe was fed up with those other four team members who always created more work for him. With Tim on board, Joe's life at work has been a lot easier!

Another six months pass. Tim has been with you for a year. Plus, with your employee referral incentive program, he has recommended two more A-Players whom you have hired. You are kicking back, pleased with yourself that in one year's time, you've let four really bad team members go and replaced them with three A-Players. Your profits have doubled. You have been able to go after three times the amount of work you had in the previous year and are generating a lot more revenue—with fewer team members! What's more, since you cut the slackers from your team, costs have gone down considerably.

You reflect on this and decide you want to do something really nice for Joe. After all, Joe helped you get the ball rolling in the right direction by recommending Tim to you. You've noticed Joe looking at travel magazines on his breaks. You ask him about that. Turns out, he wants to take his wife away for a nice weekend for their anniversary. This gives you an idea. You surprise Joe with a weekend getaway at the mountain lodge a few hours from town.

This costs you less than $500 because it's the off-season. Joe is thrilled. He feels extravagantly well taken care of by you. You consider this gift a nominal token of appreciation. After all, your profits have doubled in the last year!

Joe now sings your praises to everyone he encounters. Tim and his buddies do the same. They've all benefited from the employee referral incentive program. You have great applicants chomping at the bit to come to work for you. But you are selective. You only hire the best.

Employee referral incentive programs are easy to install and produce quick results. If you are in need of team members right now, I recommend you start with this recruiting strategy. I've seen it work time and again. It's a great strategy to quickly fill open positions with very good team members.

Expanding Your Referral Program

Expand your referral program beyond team members. Consider offering incentives to friends, family, former team members, vendors, etc. The more people you let into your referral program, the greater your reach and the better chance you have of getting the best team members.

Often Overlooked Sources for Employee Referrals[53]

- Call former A-Players who left you and ask them for referrals. Maybe they've met A-Players since leaving your business. Who knows? Maybe they are not happy in their new job and would like to come back to work for you.
- Consider A-Player team members who have retired as well as those who left their job with you to go to school or raise children. They may want to work part-time to fill in while you fill the open position, or they may know someone to refer to you.

53 - Kleiman, Mel, *100 + 1 Top Tips, Tools & Techniques to Attract & Recruit Top Talent,* Humetrics, 2010.

- Don't forget to consider your customers. Let them know about position openings. Your best customers can be great referral sources. Who knows? One of your best customers may want to work for you!

You get the idea. Tap into your networks to get more qualified applicants for a position. Call anyone you know who may know someone like the person you are seeking to hire. The more specific you are in describing the personal qualities you are seeking, the more likely you are to trigger the person you are talking to think of someone they know.

For example, instead of saying, "I am looking to hire a receptionist. Do you know of anyone looking for work," you might say: "I'm looking to fill a receptionist position. I'd like to hire someone who is warm and friendly, who is great at putting people at ease, and who pays attention to the little things that matter. Who comes to mind?"

Remember, A-Players are hardly ever out of work. So, if you ask someone in your network, "Who is looking for work?" their A-Player connections may not come to mind.

There are some important subtleties to crafting an effective referral program that many overlook. One important consideration is that you will want to build your network of people interested in the possibility of working for you now . . . and later. The reality is that many will not be ready to make the leap from their current job to work with you. But, they may in the future. So, you will want to have a systematic way to stay in touch. This is such an important part of your Hire the Best A-Player Attraction System™ that I created a short video tutorial for how to do this effectively. You can access it at *www.TapThePotential. com/Toolkit.*

Getting Team Members Involved in the Community Is a Plus for Your Business

Anytime your team members are out and about in your community, they are conducting public relations for your business. They are interacting with people who may be future team members for you.

Educate your team members to properly represent and promote your business in the community. Exceptional team members want to work for enterprises with professional reputations.

Encourage your A-Players to be involved in the community so they get to meet more A-Players. This is especially important for team members who have moved into the area to work for you. You want to help them establish deep, strong roots in your community. They are much more likely to stay! The extra benefit of doing this is that your team members build their networks of A-Players.

Mike Bailey, President of Bailey Enterprises shares, "We invested in a really nice uniform for our employees to help our employees feel they are part of the overall enterprise and raise our visibility with our customers. Our employees are very easily recognizable in the community. Your employees leave work, they go out into the community, they're going home after work in their uniform, or stopping off at the store in their uniform. They're representing your business. People are watching them working or walking down the grocery store aisle. Many of the people they run into are going to be current or future customers, or future employees."

Take this a step further by turning your team members into recruiters for you while they are out and about in the community.

Equip your team members with a business card that they can give to A-Players they encounter. In addition to the employee's contact information, include your direct contact information. On the back, include a few bullet points about what makes you an Employer of Choice for A-Players working for you.

Mike Bailey likes to acknowledge good service with the card he hands out in the community:

I noticed you doing a great job! Are you looking for new opportunities? We've been looking for you...

- Competitive Wages
- Simple IRA
- Vacation/Sick Days
- Advancement Opportunities
- Drug FREE work environment
- Insurance; medical, dental, optical

Every time I go to a restaurant, a fast food joint, or a grocery store, and I see somebody giving good service . . . an upbeat, positive employee, I'll hand them my card and say, 'We're always looking for good people.' At a minimum, you're giving that person a pat on the back and telling them they're doing a good job. Let's face it, none of us do that enough.

When one of my employees does this in the community, it makes more of an impression. It has way more value coming from a team member of the company than it does coming from me as the owner. If a team member is saying, 'Hey, this is a great place to work; we'd like to have you here,' that means a ton to them. It has way more value than me telling them that because they think I might just be blowing smoke and complimenting them because I want more employees, which I do. But I'm also not going to hand these cards to people I don't think would be good employees.

Chuck Parmely of Overhead Door Company of Riverton-Lander gives this card to his team members to share in the community:

THIS CARD COULD CHANGE YOUR LIFE!

At Overhead Door Company we notice people like you!

The person giving you this card thinks you could be a good fit for our team.

You may not want to change jobs right now, but who knows what the future holds. Just hang on to this card. When you are seriously thinking of a change, come by and see me.

Work With Schools

Think long-term when you are filling your pipeline of A-Players. You can work with schools to build relationships with students interested in pursuing trades.

You could do this in several ways. Develop relationships with local colleges and trade schools. The next generation of salespeople, professionals, office workers, and tradespeople are learning there. Teach continuing education courses or volunteer as a guest speaker in classes with students who will eventually have the skills you are seeking. Make your contact information available for students. Stick around after class, and chat with the students.

Collect contact information from any who impress you. Stay in touch! Although you may not hire this person immediately, you are building a network of A-Players. Who knows? That student may be a future employee for you, or they may refer a friend or family member to work for you.

You can also create intern opportunities for students. Establish relationships and assess their possibilities as potential future team members.

Working with schools is an excellent strategy for filling professional positions. You'll also build relationships with professors and instructors who can connect you with former students.

Tony Mancini sees the push for younger generations to go to college over pursuing skilled labor positions.[54] Tony runs the Building Group of SGC Horizon, which publishes *Professional Builder, Professional Remodeler, Building Design+Construction, PRODUCTS, Custom Builder,* and *Multifamily Design+Construction*, along with their websites and conferences.

Tony has a front-row seat to the latest industry news and trends. From his seat behind many of the biggest construction industry trade publications, Tony witnesses the impact of the labor shortage on the industry.

Tony recommends companies use innovative strategies targeted to recruiting and training skilled labor. The Skilled Labor Fund is one example of such an innovative program. The Skilled Labor Fund is part of the National Housing Endowment, a 501(c)(3) Foundation and 98.5% of all funds raised

---

54 - With the average age of skilled labor workers increasing, organizations have placed a much greater emphasis in recruiting now than any other time in memory. Many times, this means making pursuing trade work a more attractive alternative to a college education, as discussed in a report posted on This Old House's website *(https://www.thisoldhouse.com/ideas/building-skills-generation-next)*. For example, the United Association union of plumbers, fitters, welders, and service techs, or UA, is under mandate to replace 20% of their members, who are aging. One way they are doing so is by marketing their apprenticeship as the equivalent of receiving a full-ride academic or sports scholarship to a top university. Their program is free. The apprentice is paid for their full-time work. They also receive benefits right away and start accruing pension and 401(k) benefits after a probationary period, usually six months. Other associations are promoting on social media and reaching out to parents and educators. Jennifer Mefford, director of business development for the labor management effort of International Brotherhood of Electrical Workers (IBEW) Local 58 and National Electrical Contractors Association (NECA) in Detroit, and a recruitment consultant for the construction industry is trying to shift conversations parents and teenagers are having about the construction industry. She points out that an "electrician can make as much money as an electrical engineer." Moreover, during a five-year IBEW and NECA program, "an apprentice will earn $225,000 in wages and benefits—in stark contrast to a college student taking on debt to earn a four-year degree."

While this does not solve our recruitment problem, it is important to note the emphasis on the conversations these organizations are having. With crippling student loan debt being discussed more openly than ever, making money in the trades while avoiding accumulating thousands of dollars in debt makes a substantial case for people to consider construction careers as an alternative to college.

are spent on the Foundation's mission "to attract and train those who have the passion and the desire to work in [the residential construction] industry. Through student scholarships, accredited trade schools, and training facilities throughout the U.S., we're building a foundation for a stronger workforce for today and tomorrow."[55]

The Skilled Labor Fund partners with several influential associations and organizations. They support, oversee, and promote growth and best practices of the construction industry. This group includes the National Association of Home Builders, the National Association of the Remodeling Industry, the National Kitchen & Bath Association, the National Housing Endowment, Scranton Gillette Communications/SGC Horizon, and Hydrogen.[56]

Don't be afraid to think outside of the box. For example, Colorado homebuilder Oakwood Homes started a foundation to fund the Colorado Homebuilding Academy, a nonprofit organization to provide free eight-week homebuilding bootcamps to encourage new workers to enter the construction field and work with them.

During the eight weeks, they teach students how to saw, tile, drill, plaster, and paint—all the skills they'll need to build a house. In an interview with CNBC, CEO Patrick Hamill noted, "Every single year, the labor situation has basically gotten worse. People retire, and there's nobody to replace them, and as an industry, ultimately we've just done a lousy job marketing our opportunities to young people."[57]

Oakwood partners with trade associations and other homebuilders to entice young workers. "We all know if we don't do this, we're not going to have a labor force to meet the needs of our industry," Hamill noted.

This innovative approach and partnership is just one way companies can work together to fill their need for labor.

Home Builders Institute (HBI) and SkillsUSA train people pursuing skilled-labor careers. The Institute provides training, curriculum

55 - *http://www.skilledlaborfund.org/*

56 - *http://www.skilledlaborfund.org/partners.html*

57 - *https://www.cnbc.com/2017/10/31/desperate-for-workers-a-colorado-homebuilder-starts-a-free-school.html*

development, and job-placement services. Its training programs are taught in communities across the country to at-risk youth, veterans, transitioning military, justice-involved, and displaced workers.[58] Companies can register with HBI to post job openings and search its resume database for people who have completed HBI training and are looking for jobs in the building industry.[59]

SkillsUSA is a national membership association serving high school, college, and middle school students who are preparing for careers in trade, technical, and skilled service occupations.[60] As SkillsUSA describes it:

> *SkillsUSA offers local, state, and national opportunities for students to learn and practice personal, workplace, and technical skills. These three components compose the SkillsUSA Framework, a blueprint for career readiness. Local chapters conduct a full program of work, and many students also attend a district or state conference.[61]*

Businesses can look to SkillsUSA for talent or get involved through financial aid, in-kind contributions, and involvement of people in SkillsUSA activities. That doesn't just support the next generation of workers. Getting involved can provide great networking opportunities for you and your company.

Organizations like HBI and SkillsUSA are working hard to provide qualified workers for the industry. ***They are looking for employers to place their graduates.***

Tony points out that it's important to recognize the person will have a base level of education but will still need on-the-job training:

> *You have to make sure that you're continuing that training, that you're helping them and mentoring them in what you do and what you*

58 - *http://www.hbi.org/*

59 - *https://hbi.jobboardhq.com/employer/info*

60 - *https://www.skillsusa.org/about/overview/*

61 - *https://www.skillsusa.org/about/overview/*

think is important. You must continue skills training once they're on the job. It's a great way for people to have a base education level, and then you personalize it to your business on what you would want them to do.

He continues to explain that this is still an advantage because most of the time you have to start from scratch and teach them everything:

I think what you're going to get from these people are two things. You're going to get someone who has raised their hand, that wants to be part of the industry, which is a big deal in today's world—because that's one of the biggest barriers, is if you want to bring someone into construction for the first time, there's a risk after three months or six months or nine months, they're like, 'I don't want to do it. I thought I did, but I don't.'

If you know someone's already raised their hand and they're kind of self-nominating, saying, 'Hey, I want to do this,' that success rate of keeping them within the industry has to be better, and then your failure rate of losing somebody for a small business goes way down.

The second thing you would get by working with people coming in through HBI or SkillsUSA is someone with a base level of construction knowledge:

Is it exactly what you want? Probably not, but at least you know that they've been trained in the basic skills of what's going on in construction. When you do bring someone on board, having a big brother or a mentor or something watching after that person is going to be pretty key to not only getting them on board but getting them up to speed and keeping them on board.

Hiring for Growth

Cedar Ridge Log Homes is a growing, family-owned business. Andrew, Andy, Sam, and Peggy Tvardzik have lots of opportunity to grow the business and are planning ahead to fill positions. They know the attributes and skills needed to start the job as well as the skills the team member will need to develop within the first year. This is the description they shared with local school faculty:

Cedar Ridge Log Homes is looking for A-Players in all positions. The term *A-Players* is defined by us as employees that are teachable, ready to advance their skill set and influence. At Cedar Ridge, we treat every employee with the respect they deserve. We run a clean, professional, high-quality job site. We enjoy our jobs and the people we work with. We teach skills that match our natural gifts and talents. We create a great place to work. We are looking to hire potential skill. Starting pay at $12 per hour with opportunity to increase. At this time, we need two helpers that show potential in two areas, trim and framing. We structure our job site so that each person has a "specialty." We believe a team is strongest when each member participates in their natural area of expertise. We do not follow the typical "Leadman, Carpenter, Helper" job site structure.

Helper with potential future Trim Carpenter attributes:
- Detail oriented
- Enjoys bringing a job to completion
- Enjoys making sure the punch list is taken care of and prioritized
- Sees a large task and is not overwhelmed
- Can't get bogged down in the details
- Efficient use of time

Skills expected to develop over the next 12 months:
- Able to read and follow blueprints thoroughly, especially kitchen layouts
- Able to install kitchen cabinets independently
- Able to trim out entire house off blueprints
- Able to hang interior and exterior doors
- Able to set windows

Helper with potential future Framing Carpenter attributes:
- Goal oriented
- Fast, efficient, on-to-the-next-task mentality
- Likes to get the ball rolling
- Production oriented

Skills expected to develop over the next 12 months:
- Able to frame house and interior walls with only the blueprints
- Able to cut rafters
- Able to frame dormers
- Able to construct exterior decks

Develop Your Own Self-Contained Training Program

Identify a specific part of your process that continues to be vulnerable due to a lack of labor. You have an opportunity to innovate and solve a problem for yourself that may become a solution for others.

Larry Green's company, System Pavers, is a prime example of the effectiveness of having a self-contained training program. Larry created System Pavers University.[62] It is an "on-site, year-round facility which provides

---

62 - *https://systempavers.com/whyus/spu.aspx*

hands-on training, instruction, and continued education" to the entire System Pavers team.

Developing your own training program is a long-term plan. You will need to attract people into it and then train them. But you can train your entire team to use best practices and improve efficiency and consistency.

You can also use your training program as a marketing and recruitment tool for your company. System Pavers features System Pavers University on several pages of its website to achieve that effect. System Pavers University is on its Career page as a benefit to candidates.[63] It is on its About Us page to let potential candidates and customers know they take training seriously.[64] System Pavers University also has its own page on the System Pavers website.[65]

Your program does not have to be complicated. You can start with a curriculum featuring your Immutable Laws, best practices, and ways you are innovating to meet client needs.

Take Training to a Whole New Level

As you train your team and improve performance, you might consider opening your training to the public.

It might seem counterintuitive to train people with no guarantee they will work for your company. So why do that? It will likely generate many direct and indirect benefits to your company. You could attract students directly to your company. You could also gain press, as Oakwood did. That could attract more positive attention and position you as an Employer of Choice in your community. Consider opening your program to outsiders or sponsoring independent training like Oakwood does.

Train Your Team in What It Means to Be a Valued Team Member in a Small Business

Mike Bruno points out that the industry has created a pool of employees

---

63 - *https://systempavers.com/page/careers*

64 - *https://systempavers.com/whyus/default.aspx*

65 - *https://systempavers.com/whyus/spu.aspx*

who don't understand what it takes to be an efficient team member in a small business:

We have a couple of different electricians we use. Over a six-month period, one electrician hired an employee, fired him for lack of performance, another electrician we use hired and fired him, and a third electrician hired him. When you think about that, you're looking at a shrinking pool of qualified help. It's like a washing machine. These guys are just circulating around and around and around, and I think that's important to think about, because I'm of the mindset that I don't believe people intentionally do things wrong.

Take this electrician, for example. I spoke to the gentleman several times. He maybe had a little bit of an attitude issue or had some issues that maybe he should be thinking about things differently. But I don't think he was intentionally trying to not perform. As a business owner, we're running around crazy, thinking about the next place, the next place, the next place. When there's a lack of performance, we automatically think it's that employee. Sometimes it is. Sometimes it is not.

As the business owner, you have to take full responsibility for everything, and there's no excuse beyond yourself. I don't believe we're responsible for the accountability of the employee, but many of these people have not been properly trained or educated in a 25- or 30-year career about how to act as an employee working for a construction business in a small business environment. Many of them have developed a sense of entitlement, and the entitlement is compartmentalized into a 'What am I making per day?' mindset.

Forget about thinking, 'I want to help this contractor build this electrical company; I want to be part of it; I want to be a journeyman electrician and then move up to project management, and I want to maybe make $120,000 a year and help him and retire from this company.' They just want to know, 'Am I making $180 a day, $200 a day, or $225 a day?' But we can change those conversations by giving them the proper training and direction they have lacked for so long.

Mike's experience is common in the construction industry. Train your team to understand best practices and how their work fits into your greater business. This is key to creating a great place to work that attracts A-Players to your business. The challenges many construction business owners face is finding the time to deliver this training as well as struggling with how to convey these concepts in a way that team members respond and take ownership of the important role they play in the business. I'm helping business owners like you bridge that training gap through Tap the Potential's Leadership Bootcamp. The bootcamp helps team members shift from thinking, *What am I making today? to How can I improve my performance for the customer, my business, and me?* We help team members find purpose beyond their paycheck. You can learn more at *www.TapThePotential.com/Leadership*.

Growing Weeders Into Leaders

A colleague of mine, Jeff McManus, wrote a book called *Growing Weeders Into Leaders, Leadership Lessons from the Ground Up* (Morgan James, 2018). Jeff is the director of Landscape Services at Ole Miss University. When he got to Ole Miss, the campus was *ugly*. The Landscape Services Department wasn't performing well at all. They would just go through the motions, pull weeds, mow lawns, and trim trees. They took no pride in their work, and it showed.

Jeff needed to improve results. With a team who looked at themselves as simply weed pullers (or, as Jeff calls them, "weeders"), improving results would not be easy. But Jeff decided to use basic leadership principles to attempt to transform his team of *weeders* into a team of *leaders*. Jeff understood that each of us is a leader. No matter where we are in the corporate ladder, we all lead. The first person each of us needs to lead is ourselves.

Whether you are the CEO or at the bottom of the organization chart, before you lead others, you must first lead yourself. One of the best ways to start leading yourself is to understand the true purpose and impact your work has on the company.

Jeff learned 62% of college applicants who visit a school make a decision about whether they want to attend it within the first few minutes. The number-one influence on that decision is how the campus looks—the architecture and landscaping.

When Jeff learned this, he knew he had come across something with the potential to be impactful. While it was not like flipping a switch and finding true production, he talked with his team about the impact their work has. "Look, the people who come here are going to be curing cancer. They're going to be building the best companies. They're going to be employing people," Jeff said. "We have an opportunity to help foster the next generation of leaders by attracting them to our campus. Sixty-two percent of the people who come here will make a decision based on how beautiful this place is, and we can make this place more beautiful so we can have the next face transplant surgeon come through our university."

From that point on, the landscape services workers no longer saw their work as pulling weeds or mowing grass. They were building a campus that could get the person who cures cancer to attend their university.

Jeff did something incredible at Ole Miss, something I bet many people thought impossible. The results were more than visual. In the years since he joined, Ole Miss' campus went from eyesore to winning "most beautiful campus" awards, of course. But his team achieved those results with *fewer* people and a *smaller* budget.

His results were so dramatic he was asked to train other

departments and other companies on how he "grew weeders into leaders" through a curriculum he developed called Landscape University.

Jeff is a great example of someone who helped his team look beyond their paycheck to the greater impact of their work. He lit a fire under his people. He reset their mindset. He re-trained their brains to focus not on what they were putting into their work but what impact they were making.

The same is true in the construction industry. If your team members see their work as spackling, sanding floors, or hanging drywall, they will find it hard to do much beyond the bare minimum. But when they go into a house and say, "People are going to have family dinners here. Their Christmas tree is going to go there," their entire perspective and motivation shifts. It's really fascinating—that mindset shift. Many assume it doesn't apply to blue collar workers. They think "We're just building buildings" or "We just hang cabinets." The truth is all the work you do is much more important than that.

I interviewed Jeff on the *Profit by Design* podcast, which I've included in the accompanying Toolkit at *www. TapThePotential.com/Toolkit*.

Train Your Team About Your Mission, Vision, and Acceptable Behavior

We've identified what we want to be when we grow up. We've also identified what we don't want to be when we grow up. As we do that, we then start to realize what kind of people we want to surround ourselves with.

Because we know what we don't want to be, we can identify what's a good fit. We can do coaching and give performance feedback to individuals in a very, very significant way. And it's not so subjective, because we know what we want to be when we grow up, and we know what we don't want to be. We can help people grow inside of the organization—from both a growth standpoint and a fit standpoint.

I think what happens in companies often is they spend a lot of time coming up with their mission and vision, and that's great. But those are talking points.

More important—or at least equally important to mission and vision—are *behaviors*. So if this is our mission, and this is our vision, what does that mean as far as behavior goes? So *how do we want people to behave?* And I think that's the third bucket that's often missed.

—Brian Gottlieb

Tuition or Student Loan Repayment Programs

Consider offering a student loan repayment program. You build loyalty with employees while offering a perk your competitors may not offer.

Many professions already use and benefit from student loan repayment programs. Teachers, social workers, physical therapists, nurse practitioners, psychologists, and physicians are just a few. Typically, they offer repayment benefits in exchange for a commitment to serve in an underserved area for a specified period of time.

You can structure a tuition reimbursement program for approved courses, or a student loan repayment program.

Making student loan payments tends to be stressful for employees. A modest tuition reimbursement or student loan repayment benefit feels more valuable than the same amount in salary.

In fact, this is how I came to move to Riverton, WY, from Austin, TX, upon completing my doctoral degree. I was a psychologist working in an underserved area for a two-year commitment, so the National Health Service Corps paid off my student loans. When I considered the interest that would have compounded on those loans over the years, it was like winning the lottery! I also stayed much longer than my two-year commitment.

You might not pay off student loans in their entirety for your team members. You might structure a program that rewards them for loyalty to your team with payments toward student loans. For example, they may earn a percentage of the profit after being with you for three years. At that point, that money could be put in an account held in the name of the business and designated for the team member. Withdrawals from that account could be used to pay off student loans. Calculate the interest you will save them from this type of program. Put it on paper and show them. It's eye-opening for your team members and you!

Be a Disrupter to Stand out as an Employer of Choice

Brian Gottlieb shared several insights with me about how he and Tundraland work to stand out in a competitive employment market:

One of the things we do as a point of differentiation is look for pain points in the market and say, 'Okay, how can we be a disruptor?'

We ask, 'How do we be a disruptor in the way we do business?' or 'How do we be a disruptor in the way we hire? The way we train? How do we change the norm? How do we become different?'

What typically happens in most organizations is a construction company gets a resume. It's sent to the business owner. The business owner is out meeting with customers or meeting with future jobs or talking

> *with his crews. So it might be that night or the next day before he actually gets a chance to review the resume and give the person a call. When they get on the phone, they do some interviewing and all that typical stuff. There's usually a twenty-four-hour lag time.*
>
> *We look at gathering resumes like we do lead generation. When we put an ad or do a television commercial and the phone rings, we answer right away. We schedule an appointment right way. We want to get in the home and make a sale.*
>
> *We treat recruitment the same way, with that same level of urgency. So, that's the first thing we do. When we get a resume, we review it and call the candidate within seconds. That is the first thing we do.*
>
> *The second thing we do as a point of differentiation is create creative compensation structures. A lot of talented people here in Wisconsin went to the UW school systems and left with a whole bunch of student loans. And these kids, these young, talented minds don't care so much about how much money they make because they have this weighing anchor around them in their student loans. So, we craft compensation structures that help pay down their student debt for them.*
>
> *These are just two of the things that help us stand out in the market.*

Acquisitions and Downsizing

Do you know of any businesses in your area that are going through a merger, acquisition, or downsizing? Team members in those businesses are typically stressed by the changes. This is particularly true if it's a hometown business being acquired by an outside corporation. Team members fear losing their ability to serve their customers in the friendly way they've enjoyed. Corporate policy often tramples family business values. This is a prime time to network with A-Players in these businesses and let them know about the opportunities you offer. This is the time to emphasize job stability and your business's values. Who knows? You might pick up a few new team members.

Work With Other Businesses

Develop cooperative relationships with other business owners who have Immutable Laws like yours. When you have openings, ask if they have any great applicants they did not hire. Reciprocate when you receive applications from A-Players you do not hire.

This is a particularly good option for businesses with seasonal needs for team members. If you can identify a business that has a peak season opposite of yours, you may be able to share team members. This is a win-win-win situation. You are developing a strong relationship with a fellow business owner who can send business your way and vice versa. Plus, your team members can be employed year-round. They will appreciate not having to scramble for work in the off-season. Further, you are less likely to lose them to another employer when they find work in the off-season.

This type of cooperative relationship can also pay off as you grow. Perhaps you can't offer full-time employment for a role that needs to be filled because it would drive down the profitability of your company. However, you are able to offer part-time employment. Partnering with another growing company with similar needs can allow you to share team members.

If other businesses don't have team members you can take on directly, consider a subcontracting relationship with them.

Get Seasonal Help Coming Back Over and Over

If you use seasonal help, give the A-Players a partial bonus for signing on for the next season before the end of this season. Give them the rest of the bonus a few weeks into the next season.

Use your seasonal people when regular team members are on vacation or you have sudden increased demand from customers.

Send Your Team Members on the Road to Recruit for You

When you send your team members to conferences or trade shows, remind them to be on the lookout for A-Players. Send them with a stack of your referral cards.

Ask your team members to come back with names and contact information for at least three or four people who might be great team members for you. If you have an employee referral incentive program, your team members will be more than happy to do this.

When the team members come back, follow up quickly with any contacts they made.

Introduce yourself immediately with a short, handwritten note. Mention the name of the employee who mentioned them to you. Consider including a brief article, tip, or resource that could benefit the other person.

To stay in touch with these referrals, be sure to add them to your database. If you have a company newsletter, ask if you can subscribe them to your newsletter. This is a great way to stay in touch and share your company culture with them. When you have openings, you can advertise through your company newsletter and often fill openings on the spot.

Publicize Your A-Players

Feature your A-Players in your company newsletter, local news media, and social media. Feature your best people, where they came from, how they got their jobs, why they stay, and why they love their jobs. Your customers will love getting to know your team members, and this puts a human face on your business. Your team members will be excited to share these posts with their friends on social media.

Have you promoted from within? Send out a press release. Build your reputation as an employer who provides opportunities for team members to advance their careers.

The added benefit: A-Players are reading! You will be piquing their interest in working for you.

Help the Family

When recruiting an A-Player who will be moving into your area, address the needs, concerns, and hesitations of their spouse and children. A move to a new town is a significant life stressor, even when it brings a pay raise and improvement in quality of life.

Many a business owner experiences problems "importing" talent into their business. If you don't address the fears and concerns of the spouse and children, your candidate may disappear. Or worse, start only to leave because their spouse couldn't find work or children couldn't adjust.

When a new A-Player team member is moving from out of town, help their spouse find work. Also, find out their interests, and help the family get integrated into the community.

A-Players hang together; the spouse of your new A-Player employee is likely to be an A-Player. Helping the spouse find work makes it likely your A-Player will stick around.

Helping a fellow business owner by sending them a potential A-Player applicant is a win-win-win! They may return the favor in the future.

Find Their Hot Buttons

What else is important to your prospective team members? Find out what matters to them, and show them how working for you will help them achieve these things.

Erika Taylor is director of content for *Professional Remodeler*. Through that role, she has learned what Millennials want and how construction companies can appeal to them. In her words, "Millennials are about more than the money. They want that flexible work schedule. They want the ability to bring their rabbit into the office. They want to align themselves with a company that's doing some kind of social good."

If you're looking to attract the next generation of workers, add flexibility, fun, and purpose-driven elements to your work. Be clear with Millennial candidates about these creative things you offer. Let them know how your company gives back to the community and contributes to some kind of social good. Be specific about how their work will help further those efforts.

Include these items in your job postings. Let Millennials know working with your company aligns with their hot buttons.

Look Into Underrepresented and Nontraditional Sources of Construction Laborers

When I spoke with Ronda Conger, one thing that stood out was how effective she has been at tapping into a network of female A-Players to build her staff. At the time of the interview, her staff was about 65% women.

Ronda is not alone. Sundance Construction Co. of Springfield, Missouri, includes an all-female framing crew.[66] The company's CEO was especially impressed with how detail-oriented his female team members are. He notes that details matter greatly in construction for both safety and customer satisfaction.

The statistics vary, but there is no doubt women are underrepresented in the construction industry. Women make up about half the total U.S. labor force but approximately 9% of construction workers, according to the Bureau of Labor Statistics. That number shrinks to about 2.5% when it comes to construction laborers.[67] Part of the labor shortage solution could lie in this underrepresented group.

The construction industry offers many advantages to other industries for female workers. Women in the U.S. earn on average 81.1% of what men make, according to the National Association of Women in Construction (NAWIC). The gender pay gap is much narrower in the construction industry. In construction, women earn on average 95.7% of what men make.[68] Although there's still a gap to bridge, the construction industry offers a much smaller distance to pay equality.

The higher average pay makes construction an attractive alternative to other industries. With an average starting wage being $60,000 a year with no experience, more and more women are considering careers in construction.[69]

The lower-than-average pay gap combined with the advantages of becoming an Employer of Choice, training your team well, and putting into

66 - https://www.ky3.com/content/news/All-female-crew-helping-break-down-gender-barriers-in-world-of-construction-492903531.html

67 - https://www.dol.gov/wb/occupations_interactive.htm

68 - https://www.nawic.org/nawic/statistics.asp

69 - https://www.channel3000.com/news/build-like-a-girl-summer-program-exposes-teenage-girls-to-construction-jobs/779342468

place clear Immutable Laws can make a well-run construction company highly attractive to women. Women are likely to be one of the greatest areas for growth in the construction industry. The NAWIC started fundraising to put together a full-length documentary called Hard Hatted Women.[70] *For Construction Pros* suggests women can be the solution to the construction industry's labor shortage if given the chance.[71]

If you continue to struggle to find A-Players, look for opportunities to bring more women onto your team.

What To Do if You Can't Find That A-Player

Sometimes it is difficult to find an A-Player. That does not mean all hope is lost. Take a look at your current team members. Can some of their tasks be automated, outsourced, or eliminated? This can free them up to assume some or all of the duties for the position you're having a hard time filling with an A-Player.

Do you have a clearly defined niche? Have you identified a clear sweet spot in your business that intersects the needs of your top clients and customers with the strengths of your team and your most profitable services and products? Our team strategizes with business owners to right-size the business around a highly profitable sweet spot. We then restructure roles of existing team members around that sweet spot. Many business owners who thought they needed more team members come to realize they actually need fewer team members to run more profitably (and with a lot fewer headaches!).

Could you restructure to do more with fewer team members?

Could you invest in newer or better training or tools to help your team do more in less time?

---

70 - *http://www.hardhattedwoman.com/* (To donate visit *https://www.gofundme.com/nawic*)

71 - *https://www.forconstructionpros.com/blogs/construction-Toolkit/blog/21022942/lets-fill-the-construction-labor-shortage-with-women*

Think Flexibly

Not every role in your small business requires a full-time person. Mike Bruno focuses on developing a core group of team members and then hiring task-specific assistants:

> *There's one in the office and two in the field that are certainly core players. They understand the drive. They understand the mission. They understand how everything works. They're accountable for what their job function is, so I don't need to micromanage the details. We have the established 'why,' why they're here and what they're doing, and then, depending on which position it is, we work with these outside assistants in these different capacities, and it works well.*
>
> *When I say assistant, we put things out there that are a lower paying rate, and we make it super flexible, work from home, Zoom meetings, and it's great. It follows that gig economy model. Somebody could have a full-time job, and they have five extra hours a week, and they want to do something for $15 an hour. They look at it as, 'It's my car payment or half of my car payment, or my kid's gymnastics. I'll do it, no problem.'*

Break Down the Role to Fill Even the Most Challenging Positions to Hire For

Mike Bruno had a difficult time trying to find a production coordinator. As he explained it:

It's been quite some time since we've been able to fulfill that role in its entirety the way that it should be, and it's such an important part of a construction company. We've tried recruiting firms. We've tried raising salaries beyond what, really, the position should be paid, and, systemically, we're finding that either you have an underqualified person seeing the dollar amount and trying to go after the job, or you have a qualified person who wants double because they're used to working for a much larger company.

So, if you're a project manager and you went to college or have any level of experience, do you really want to work for a very small remodeling firm somewhere? Or do you want to work for one of the big boys, where you're going to have wide experience and more opportunities? Here's what Mike did:

We've had to break the position down into smaller plates, if you will, and say, 'Let's look at the different components of this position, and can we move some of these key components to different assistants to be able to do it?' As an example, a project manager should be able to perform some level of estimating. They're performing customer engagement and customer discussions, scheduling, subcontracting negotiation, budgeting, things like that.

We've had to push some of the subcontracting negotiation and the budgeting to accounting staff, and then we've had to push some of the estimating to part-time estimators that we work with, so we found estimators that work for those larger companies that are looking to make some extra money, and then we've pushed some of the field-level management to the couple core guys that we have.

We've had to learn to seek out better subcontractors that have a higher level of professionalism that don't need much hand-holding, which is also a struggle, but that's kind of where we've been with it.

Stay in touch!

We've covered a lot of strategies to connect with A-Players. It all comes down to building a chain of connections with A-Players and staying in touch. After all, it does no good to do all of this networking if you don't stay in touch. Your contacts go cold. The next time you have an open position, you'll be right back where you started—filling it based on who responds to your ad at the local job service office.

Start a database of good quality people you encounter, whom you would consider hiring. Create ways to stay in touch. Send holiday cards, birthday cards, articles, newspaper clippings, etc. Stay top of mind!

If you have a company newsletter, keep former team members on your mailing list. This is a great way to gently remind them of the opportunities you offer and why you are an Employer of Choice. Mention your employee referral incentive program, so they can continue to refer to you long after they've moved on.

Connect with A-Players you know via LinkedIn and Facebook. See who A-Players are connected with, and discover their professional groups. This is another avenue to explore for A-Players.

Also, ask your best team members what social media platforms they use most. It would be good to have a presence on those sites to help you stay top of mind in their networks.

At Tap the Potential, we help our clients identify the simplest, most effective, and profitable strategies for their needs. We identify what works for your business. Then we help you systemize it so you have a steady stream of qualified candidates inquiring about working for you—an Employer of Choice.

The world is full of A-Players who are passionate about the work they do. All they need is a great place to work. If you do not invest in this, you will be doing a great disservice to your current and potential team members, customers, and, of course, yourself.

Your team members will suffer because they will have less support and direction. Your future customers will suffer as well. Their projects will be performed by unmotivated B- or C-Players, or worse, using second-tier technology. You will suffer because you will have to work harder, earn less, and have less impact in your home, company, and community.

Get out of our own way, fight through the bad days, and create that great place to work A-Players demand.

> **"Keep your chin up. Keep moving forward. You've got this!"**

It doesn't matter what your past experiences are. You can't change the past. But you can change the future, and the Hire the Best System™ can help. Use this book in your business. Take the next step and sign up for my comprehensive Hire the Best™ online course to get my guidance in fully implementing the Hire the Best System™ in your business.

To learn more and register, visit *www.TapThePotential.com/Course.*

Author's Note

Thank you for reading *How To Hire the Best*. It is my deepest desire to help you develop a business that is a highly profitable, great place to work. It allows you to experience the freedom that comes from having a business that does not depend on you to run. After all, work supports life, not the other way around. I hope *How To Hire the Best* is taking you one step closer to that experience of your business.

I'd like to ask a small favor of you. Of course, there is no obligation.

Would you be willing to post an honest review of *How To Hire the Best* on Amazon? Reviews really are the best way for others to discover this book and the solutions within. Even a sentence or two from you helps other entrepreneurs.

Your honest feedback is what's important. If you loved the book, please say so (you rock!). If you didn't like the book, say that. And, if you're feeling neutral about it, say that. What's important is that other entrepreneurs hear your truth about *How To Hire the Best*.

It takes just a few minutes and is the best way to get the word out. Search for "How To Hire the Best" in the Amazon search bar. Choose this book. Scroll down to "Customer Reviews," and click "Write a Customer Review."

I appreciate you!

Sabrina

Appendix A
Take the Next Steps with Us...

Hire the Best Online Course™

Get step-by-step implementation of the Hire the Best System™ in my online course. The course includes on-demand clinics so you can learn whenever it is convenient for you. You will learn:

- how to *quickly* hire right. Discover the most important qualities to hire for, which most business owners completely overlook.
- quick and easy strategies to tell if a candidate is the right fit.
- how to get *top candidates* to line up to work for you (even if you cannot pay top dollar).
- how to set up the ideal employee referral incentive program to tap into networks of A-Players.
- PLUS...simple and inexpensive strategies for spreading the word about the opportunity to work for you—an Employer of Choice!

To learn more about my complete course in the Hire the Best System™, visit *www.TapThePotential.com/Course*.

Tap the Potential's Exclusive Small Group Coaching Program

If you like the idea of building a great culture that attracts A-Players and are struggling to make this a reality in your business, our team is here to help! This is what we specialize in. Our Exclusive Small Group Coaching Program is designed to support you in being the leader you need to be to create a highly profitable, great place to work that allows you to take a 4 week vacation.

If you're interested in joining our program, your next step is to take our assessment of your business at *www.TapThePotential.com/Assessment*. You'll discover what to do next to make your business a highly profitable, great place to work. You'll also learn how close you are to being able to take a 4 Week Vacation. We'll invite you to meet with a member of our team to debrief your results and determine if our program is a good fit for you.

Leadership Bootcamp

Effective leaders in a small business propel the business forward by leaps and bounds. You need team members who are your allies in transforming your business into a great place to work! You need team members who leverage the greatness in themselves to be an asset to the business while tapping into the greatness in others. You need team members who understand your business, where it's going, and their role in taking it there. Your A–Player team members will get all this and more in Leadership Bootcamp.

To learn more and register team members, go to *www.TapThePotential. com/Leadership*.

Coach Approach

Imagine your team members taking initiative, thinking on their own, engaging in creative problem-solving, and making decisions. See them aligned with your Immutable Laws and serving your customers, team members, and objectives.

Envision team members at all levels engaging in open, honest, supportive communication with one another. They give supportive and critical feedback to one another. Think of teams working in harmony to achieve high goals.

Imagine **a coaching culture**. A coaching culture is about delivery, performance, accountability, and tapping into potential. It helps you achieve extraordinary outcomes.

A strong culture increases net income 765% over ten years, according to a Harvard study of more than 200 companies. In the Coach Approach Online Interactive Workshop, you will learn how to create a coaching culture.

To learn more and register, go to *www.TapThePotential.com/Coach-Approach.*

A-Player Onboarding: The Proven System for Driving Loyalty, Engagement, and Success

You've hired an A-Player, now what? Most business owners do haphazard onboarding, which can lead to rapid turnover. All that work to hire the best goes down the drain if you don't follow up with an effective onboarding and engagement plan.

From the interview to their first day, all the way through the end of the team members' first year with you and beyond . . . Get our step-by-step system for successful onboarding to drive loyalty and quickly ramp your A-Players up for success.

To learn more and register, go to *www.TapThePotential.com/Onboarding.*

Appendix B

Book Dr. Sabrina Starling to Speak at Your Next Event

Dr. Sabrina Starling will occasionally travel for keynote speaking engagements. To inquire about her availability, visit *www.TapThePotential.com/ Speaking*.

Bibliography

Burkus, David. *Friend of a Friend…: Understanding the Hidden Networks That Can Transform Your Life and Your Career.* Boston: Houghton Mifflin Harcourt, 2018.

Coyle, Daniel. "Introduction: When Two Plus Two Equals Ten." *The Culture Code: the Secrets of Highly Successful Groups*, Bantam, 2018, p. xviii.

Cusato, Marianne. "The Skilled Labor Shortage: Where is the Next Generation of Craftsmen?" *HomeAdvisor.* February, 2016.

Fleischer, Charles. *HR for Small Business: An Essential Guide for Managers, Human Resources Professionals and Small Business Owners* (2nd Edition), Sphinx Publishing , 2009.

Herold, Cameron. *Double Double: How to Double Your Revenue and Profit in 3 Years or Less.* Greenleaf Book Group LLC, 2011.

Heskett, J., W.E. Sasser Jr., and L. Schlesinger. *The Service Profit Chain: How Leading Companies Link Profit and Growth to Loyalty, Satisfaction, and Value.* New York: Free Press, 1997.

Keiningham, Timothy L., and Lerzan Aksoy. *Why Loyalty Matters: The Groundbreaking Approach to Rediscovering Happiness, Meaning and Lasting Fulfillment in Your Life and Work.* Dallas, TX: Benbella Books, 2010.

Keyser, John. "Are we happy yet: How coaching is improving workplace morale." *Choice* Volume 11, Number 4. pp 19-20, December 2013.

Kienast, MCC, CPCC, Theresa A. "Engage Employees and Become a Superhero!" *Choice*, Vol 10, Number 2.

Kleiman, Mel, *100 + 1 Top Tips, Tools & Techniques to Attract & Recruit Top Talent*, Humetrics, 2010.

Kotter, J. P., and J.L. Heskett. *Corporate Culture and Performance*. New York: Free Press, 1992.

McCarthy, Pat. "Leading Practices for the State's Secondary Career and Technical Education Programs" *Office of the Washington State Auditor*. December 19, 2017.

McManus, Jeff. *Growing Weeders Into Leaders: Leadership Lessons from the Ground Level*. New York: Morgan James, 2018.

Michalowicz, Mike. *Profit First: A Simple System to Transform Any Business from a Cash-Eating Monster to a Money-Making Machine*. Portfolio, 2017.

Michalowicz, Mike. *The Pumpkin Plan: A Simple Strategy to Grow a Remarkable Business in Any Field*. New York: Portfolio/Penguin, 2012.

Pryce-Jones, Jessica. "Positive profits: How happiness at work impacts the bottom-line." *Choice*, Volume 11, Number 4, pp 27-28.

Schneider, Benjamin, Paul J. Hanges, D. Brent Smith, and Amy Nicole Salvaggio. "Which Comes First: Employee Attitudes or Organizational Financial and Market Performance?" *Journal of Applied Psychology* 88, no. 5 (2003): 836–51. https://doi.org/10.1037/0021-9010.88.5.836

Smart, Bradford D. Topgrading: *The Proven Hiring and Promoting Method That Turbocharges Company Performance* (3rd Edition). New York: Portfolio/Penguin, 2012.

Smart, Geoff, and Randy Street. *Who: The A Method for Hiring*. New York: Ballantine Books, 2008.

About the Author

Dr. Sabrina Starling, The Business Psychologist™ and author of the *How To Hire the Best* series is the founder of Tap the Potential. Tap the Potential specializes in transforming small businesses into highly profitable, great places to work, then sending business owners on a 4 week vacation to celebrate that accomplishment.

Never one to accept status quo or back down from a challenge, Dr. Starling's *How To Hire the Best* series grew from her desire to solve hiring challenges interfering with her clients' growth and profitability. What sprang from her experience working with entrepreneurs in rural areas catapulted her to becoming the world's leading expert in attracting top talent in small businesses — no matter what hiring challenges those businesses are facing — and earned Tap the Potential's reputation as the go-to resource for entrepreneurs committed to creating great places to work with thriving coaching cultures and highly engaged team members working from strengths.

With her background in psychology and years of driving profit in small business, Dr. Starling knows what it takes to find, keep, and get exceptional performance out of your biggest investment—your team members.

Dr. Starling lives in Alexandria, Louisiana, with her two daughters at her home, the Entrepreneurs Retreat Center. There she hosts the annual Breakthroughs on the Bayou Retreats. She is a popular speaker for local, state, and national organizations and industry. When she is not writing, speaking, or coaching, she enjoys traveling, gardening, and knitting.

Visit *www.TapThePotential.com* to learn more about the life-changing transformations Dr. Sabrina and her team bring overworked business owners.

Tune in weekly to the Profit by Design podcast as Dr. Sabrina and her co-host, Mike Bruno, bring you tips, tools, and strategies to grow a sustainably profitable business that allows you to live the lifestyle you desire.

Made in the USA
Lexington, KY
24 October 2019